Reflections on Racing

Racing
Mercy Rimell

Introduced and edited by Ivor Herbert

PELHAM BOOKS
Stephen Greene Press

PELHAM BOOKS/STEPHEN GREENE PRESS

Published by the Penguin Group
27 Wrights Lane, London W8 5TZ, England
Viking Penguin Inc., 40 West 23rd Street, New York, New York 10010, USA
The Stephen Greene Press, Inc., 15, Muzzey Street,
Lexington, Massachusetts 02173, U.S.A.

Penguin Books Australia Ltd, Ringwood, Victoria, Australia
Penguin Books Canada Ltd, 2801 John Street, Markham, Ontario, Canada L3R 1B4
Penguin Books (NZ) Ltd, 182–190 Wairau Road, Auckland 10, New Zealand

Penguin Books Ltd, Registered Offices: Harmondsworth, Middlesex, England

First published 1990

Typeset by Cambrian Typesetters, Frimley in 10½/13pt Palatino
Printed and bound in Great Britain by Richard Clay, Bungay, Suffolk

ISBN 0 7207 1965 8

A CIP catalogue record for this book is available from the British Library.

Frontispiece

*Fred and me in about
1979 with a group of
horses, including Royal
Frolic on the left.*

Contents

Photo credits

The authors and publishers are grateful to the following for permission to reproduce copyright photographs: Berrows Newspapers page 111; Central Press page 17; Cheltenham Newspaper Co pages 34–35, 46; Gerry Cranham pages 119, 122, 126, 134, 139, 144, 148, 155, 159, 160; *Daily Graphic* page 49; *Express and Star* page 84; Fox Photos page 70; Graphic Photos page 76; Van Hallan page 62; Keystone pages 18, 54; Bernard Parkin pages 138, 152 (top and bottom); Provincial Press Agency pages 112, 121; Reuter page 88; W. W. Rouch and Co pages 8, 58; Sport and General pages 41, 45, 52, 66, 75, 92, 95, 97, 98, 105, 108–9, 117; *The Sun* frontispiece and page 140; A. V. Swaebe page 38.

Every effort has been made to trace copyright owners but in some cases this has not been possible.

Foreword

by Ivor Herbert

This book is a compilation of interviews with Mercy Rimell recorded over the summer of 1989, which covered the regretted end of her training career and the start of her retirement.

The views expressed – as anyone knowing Mercy will realise – are entirely hers. With some of them I strongly disagree. Others I can't support with the vehement conviction she expresses. But there they all stand.

This is her book: the reflections of an expert deeply involved in racing for fifty-two years should come out hot, strong and unadulterated.

Some of the material was taken verbatim from transcripts of interviews which Michael Tanner undertook for me on two detailed briefs I gave him. As with the rest, the words and views are entirely those of Mercy Rimell. My role was to plan the scope and format of the book, to draw her out on each subject, to put the questions, to keep her broadly on course and to edit the whole, pruning only repetitions. My aim was to keep the essence of this remarkable character down to her usual phraseology of 'obviously', 'by and large', and 'in olden times', so that the reader can clearly tell that it is Mercy Rimell speaking.

Introduction by Ivor Herbert

For more than half a century Mercy Rimell has been a redoubtable figure on British racecourses. Though she would never admit it, she is famous. Much loved by a handful of close friends with whom she's perfectly at ease, she has been generally respected in the critical world of racing. By quite a cowering few, she has been dauntingly feared. She has been described as forthright, formidable, terrifying and punningly, as merciless. It would be BBC TV journalist Julian Wilson's nightmare, I fancy, to attempt to interview her again.

She has certainly sent a few foolish media men packing. She tolerates no fools. Far from academic herself, the product of limited, then truncated schooling, she possesses a quick mind and a sharp tongue. She knows her subject. She's worked hard all her life, so she condemns indolence. From riding international class show-ponies aged seven up to training top class National Hunt horses aged seventy, she knows the horse-game hoof to withers, poll to croup. She has worked cold dawns to tired dusks throughout her life. So she condemns the ignorant who, claiming to know, talk nonsense, and the idle who haven't needed to work.

But, as so often with apparently fearless characters, Mercy's outward attitude is a metallic shield. Inside there remains, even after all her triumphs, a frightened, timid girl. She was dominated by her mother throughout her childhood. Even after her marriage at seventeen to the handsome, dashing Fred Rimell, champion NH jockey, Mercy remained in awe of Mrs Cockburn. The mother's shadow hovered darkly over all Mercy's life. It's still there. Divorced from Mercy's much-loved father, and then remarried to a kindly vet from Stratford, the powerful mother moved close to the Rimells' home and stables at Kinnersley in the green vale spreading lushly west of the Severn. She bought, unsurprisingly, an imposing residence, standing proudly on a rise above Upton-on-Severn and called The Hill. From here she could still keep an eye on Mercy. Here, in its enormous rooms commanding views over her fields, growing cattle and brood-mares and sustaining a few old equine legends, Mercy has been living since her mother's death.

It was here, in the summer of 1981, with shocking suddenness, Mercy's adored husband Fred fell dead aged sixty-eight. It was a particularly cruel time. Within a year Mercy had also lost her famous travelling head lad Jack Kidd, her indefatigable secretary Mrs Peachey, wife of a long serving Kinnersley head lad. It was acutely hard to carry on. But she was immediately supported by all her owners. And by her knowledge. The walls of The Hill are thick as autumnal leaves with the pictures of famous victories which she and Fred brought about together. Timid Mercy may be with people, but she's fearless in adversity. 'Training was the only thing I could do.'

The power of Mrs Cockburn was not exerted simply to keep control over her daughter and son. She dominated Mercy's father, too. 'And he and Fred,' says Mercy now, 'were the only two men I've ever loved and really respected.'

Mrs Cockburn had more business-like motives than mere maternal power, the refusal to let offspring fly from the nest. Mercy was a source of profit to her. Her husband farmed 500 acres by the side of Warwick racecourse. He quite liked racing and kept a few point-to-pointers without being in any way professionally involved in the sport. Indeed, with typical generosity he sold to the racecourse – for 'almost a peppercorn', Mercy recalls – an extra strip to make the Warwick straight.

Father Cockburn was a typical, sporting yeoman farmer. But his wife was deeply involved in the commercial side of the equine world. She recognised the big money to be made from small but brilliant show ponies. She had a daughter who had ridden from the age of two, and who aged five rode superbly. So the mother bought a succession of ponies. She and the child Mercy would make them, produce them, bring them out, show them in the highest class, win championships with them. Mrs Cockburn could then sell them for substantial profits.

Mercy was the essence of this business. Unlike other horsey children who grow up with ponies, loving them for years even when outgrown, Mercy's ponies were turned over double-quick and sometimes sold on the showground. She had no sooner grown fond of a pony, but it was whipped away from her. And because boarding-school would have seriously impeded Mercy's duties as the stables' star rider, Mrs Cockburn kept her at home on the job. Thus Mercy grew up without the friendships of her own school age groups. These, she still thinks, would have provided her with a large group of everlasting friends. This may only be partly true: few schoolday friendships endure the post-school separations, geographical, economic, and social. But Mercy believes it. She is convinced she lost out on friends. To this day she finds it almost impossible to approach an acquaintance. She feels she can't go into a restaurant or pub on her own. She needs people to greet her.

With typical fairness, she points out that, however poignant the parting from pony after pony, the rapid changes of ride and character, the bringing-on and bringing-out of so many different ponies, enormously improved her riding. She was, in fact, though she won't say so, a child prodigy in the saddle, as good an equestrienne of her vintage as anyone in Britain.

She was therefore grounded in ponies and horses but not in racing when, at a local Sunday tennis party, she met Fred. She was sixteen. It was pre-war. 'We didn't have television or anything like that, of course. We made our own entertainment. Tennis parties were the main way of meeting other young people.'

I had supposed she had married Fred so young partly to escape her mother's clutches. But this was no part of the reason, as Mercy saw it, and still sees it. She fell instantly in love with this attractive man, twice champion jockey before the war, and twice (once shared) after it. 'I've never looked at another man since, though' (with a twinkle) 'I've had plenty of offers!'

Her mother did not approve of the marriage, 'She didn't know any racing people and thought them, well, racey!' Mercy had another boy-friend, son of the conductor Sir Thomas Beecham, who lived locally and on whom she supposes her mother might have looked less unfavourably. Mercy was seventeen. Fred would be twenty-four the day after their June wedding.

Mercy's father continued his constant support, but could provide no dowry. Then, after a few years of Fred earning about £1 a mile riding over fences and hurdles, the war came, cutting racing back to the barest knuckle. There was no jump racing at all during the three years 1942–1944, and only a few meetings before and after. Fred Rimell's first 'post-war' championship, tying with 'Frenchie' Nicholson, was won with just fifteen winners.

The young Rimells struggled through the war. The snakes and ladders of the racing game were already there. From being the young glamorous wife of the champion jockey, Mercy was a young mother while Fred drove RAF lorries. He was insufficiently qualified to fly.

The setting in which young Mercy found herself at the western end of the Vale of Evesham had been Rimell territory since the start of the century. Fred's father Tom was the son of a local farmer. He went away to work in racing, and rose to become head lad to two Newmarket trainers. He then started on his own at Kinnersley which was part of the huge Croome Estate. The landowners then were the Earls of Coventry, whose ancestry traces back five and a half centuries to Sir Thomas Coventry, Lord Mayor of London in 1426. The present Earl sold the estate to the Sun Alliance insurance company who leased stables, cottages, gallops and about 600 acres of farmland first to Fred Rimell, and then on Fred's death to Mercy, till her lease expired in the summer of 1989. During that summer, the company's estate agents invited Mercy to sit on their selection committee, interviewing new applicants for the lease.

Fred was apprenticed at Kinnersley to his father as a tiny boy, rode his first winner aged twelve, and rode thirty-four flat race winners in his youth. With his two pre-war jockey champion-ships, Fred topped the list for the fourth and last time in the first full post-war season of 1945–6. He then broke his neck for the second time, lay paralysed for four hours and was incarcerated in a plaster cast for three months. 'The doctors said one more fall would finish me!' he drily remarked to me in 1977 when he was sixty-four. He sensibly quit riding altogether.

With an eye to the future and to supplement a precarious income, Fred had already started to train next door to Kinnersley in Severn Stoke while he was race riding. So, as peace crept out, Mercy was not only jockey's wife, but had become Fred's assistant trainer, a job she held for forty years and with increasing influence.

She assumed all the paperwork side – 'Fred could never be bothered with any of that!' She has always had a prodigious memory. This she now applied to the names and breeding of almost every horse running and, particularly, to their form. She could thus swiftly assess the opposition, knew when their own horses were 'well in' and became a dab hand at going through *The Racing Calendar* and the entry forms. Rapidly she was picking all the races for Fred's string and placing them to their best advantage. Their successes were to that important extent due to her: horses, however fit and well win nothing in the wrong races.

While Fred lived, Mercy always made all the entries. 'I never even *look* at 'em,' he told me a few years before he died. 'She tells me what races each horse has got, and I just get 'em ready for those races!' Like most truly successful people, he could afford to undersell himself.

The partnership so prospered that the stable topped the list four times between 1976 and 1980 – the last time with the then record-breaking stakes money when Comedy of Errors also broke the record for individual prize money and was nominated 'Racehorse of the Year'.

Fred Rimell's record of four different Liverpool Grand Nationals still stands. The Hon. Aubrey Hastings also trained four, the last in 1924, but his 1917 winner Ballymacad won a nineteen-runner substitute race which took place at Gatwick where now the airport sprawls. Fred's father Tom won the 1932 Grand National. Vincent O'Brien for comparison trained three consecutive winners between 1953 and 1955.

The Rimell stable won two Cheltenham Gold Cups, three Champion Hurdles and every major race in the Calendar except the Schweppes Hurdle which was for so long the great gambling feature at Newbury in February. The Rimells, unlike Ryan Price, never believed in laying out a horse specifically for such a target.

Kinnersley under the Rimells won four Mackeson Gold Cups at Cheltenham. After Mercy continued the enterprise on her own in 1981, she won the stable's third Champion Hurdle with Gaye Brief, the Waterford Crystal Stayers Hurdle with Gaye Chance and the Arkle Trophy with Gala's Image.

During her eight years in sole command she was understandably approached several times by different publishers to write her autobiography. She was kind enough to say she would like to do this with me. My indebtedness to Fred and Mercy Rimell, my great admiration for them both and my continuing affection for her, go back to March 1957 when, as a very junior trainer indeed aged thirty-one, I had contrived to win the Cheltenham Gold Cup. The Rimells were big important figures in the game. Linwell's owner, the millionaire gear, tractor and Aston-

Martin and Lagonda manufacturer David Brown, had had a horse briefly with the Rimells. They were running E.S.B. in the Gold Cup, joint third favourite after Kerstin and Pointsman. Linwell, a less obvious choice to the public but fancied and backed by ourselves at Christmastime, started at 100-9. In these circumstances for our horse to beat theirs out of the money, should have distinctly annoyed them.

But with the generosity and sportsmanship which marked both the Rimells' racing lives, Fred and Mercy were among the first to come into the winner's enclosure to congratulate us. While doing so, they heard, to their astonishment and patent disgust, David Brown remarking to me that he wouldn't stay for a drink, but we could come up to his house next Sunday for a gin-and-tonic.

Fred exploded, 'This little man has just won the Gold Cup and he's talking about a blanking gin-and-tonic next blanking Sunday! You'll come home with *us* now. And drink *champagne*!'

So the Rimells took us out, after their own defeat, for a celebratory dinner for us. The champagne flowed till dawn, when we at last drove home to tiptoe into Linwell's box to thank him again, and to convince ourselves by touching him that it had all really happened.

Over the last few years Mercy and I have talked about her book. She was characteristically adamant that she did not want 'an ordinary autobiography starting with "I remember when" and ploughing through the years . . . All that water under the bridge . . .' I was glad about that. I think her views on racing more interesting than the glowing historical record which stands proudly on its own.

So, on a variety of racing subjects, Mercy Rimell, freshly retired trainer uses her experience of fifty-two years actively engaged in the sport to give us the brisk benefit of her opinions.

On Childhood   1

I had a strange isolated childhood. Unfortunately I only went to school for three years from the age of eight until I was eleven, because I had very bad asthma. In those days no one knew how to treat asthma and it was suggested – as these things often are – that it would be a good idea if I didn't go mixing with lots of other children. So I stayed at home, and had a governess. Consequently I had virtually no school friends, because after the age of eleven I was never at school to make any. So I lived a lonely sort of a childhood. I had one brother, but he was away at public school and I was left very much to my own activities. Consequently I grew up early, before my time. I wasn't forced to grow up; I just did, because I was never mixing with people of my own age. In some ways that may have been an advantage; in other ways not, because in this day and age you go to school until you're about seventeen and you make friends and hopefully you retain them.

Both my parents were very keen on horses and my father rode in some point-to-points. In no way was he the authoritarian pre-Great War type father. He wasn't like that at all. He was a super person, and not at all strict. My mother was, but not my father. My father farmed about 500 acres and he always hunted. So did my mother and my brother. Obviously we all rode: it was just an automatic thing then that in the country as you grew up you always rode. My mother was mad keen on this showing business and a very good judge of a horse. Every year all those years I rode in a show ring, and when I got married I thought: 'I'll never ever go to another show, I'll have nothing more to do with it,' because I'd had such a fill of it.

Yet the first thing I did when my children were old enough was to go and buy a show pony for them! He was a very good one too, called Peter Pan, virtually unbeaten, who won two years running at the Royal International, I think. He was a marvellous

The 1920s and I'm riding a pony called The Sheikh in the streets of Islington outside the International Horse Show. The pony subsequently won in France and was sold to a Princess in Spain and I had to go out there with my mother to sort the pony out! I'm clutching the Cup having won the 12.2 Championship.

pony. So I went and did exactly the thing that I said I never would do! And my daughter did the same thing with her child, though she wasn't a natural rider. We had her ride side-saddle, because she didn't ride astride so well, but she won two years running riding side-saddle at the Royal Show.

Certainly I was a 'father's girl' and I've always said that Father and Fred were the only two gentlemen I've met in my life. How do you judge a gentleman? Well, to start with my father had wonderful manners. He was a *good* person, who saw no bad in anybody. You never heard him say anything wrong about anyone. He never saw any bad because he was too good. Fred was a bit the same: he never saw anything bad in anybody, and you would never hear Fred run anybody down, or be bitchy in any way, like so many men are today.

Like Fred, my father had a great sense of humour. And, like Fred, he was a great man of the country. He would have been hopeless in the city or in that sort of life. The country life he led suited him ideally, and so I was brought up that way, too. Fred also loved the country, but he was a much more sophisticated person than my father, much more worldly. Father wasn't in any way worldly or sophisticated, and I don't know, I'm sure, how he would have got on in this day and age.

He was born in Warwickshire, but the family originally were from Cumberland. My grandfather came down from Sedbergh Hall, and they settled in Warwickshire for ever after. My mother was strict. It wasn't only in childhood that I was in awe of her authority. All my life I was always in awe of my mother, but not of my father. And if I was ever in trouble – doing all sorts of stupid things – it was always my father I went to. My mother had the most wonderful dress sense and was always immaculately dressed.

There was a blacksmith's forge at the back of the castle wall in Warwick, and I spent hours in the blacksmith's shop when I should have been at school – that's why I know so much about blacksmiths and shoes.

I was always in a hurry. I used to gallop on my pony along through the streets of Warwick. Once I slipped up going round one of these hairpin bends in Castle Lane, and I got grazed knees and grazed everything. I gathered myself up and caught the pony and continued. I didn't say anything about it because I wasn't supposed to be galloping flat out on the hard road. And I was meant to be in school.

Another day my brother and I were racing round what we called a point-to-point course over some of the land at home. I had got on my one and only school coat, and my pony turned head over heels in a muddy ditch full of water, and when I clambered out I was like a drowned rat in this wretched school coat. I came back hoping I could sneak it into the house and not be seen. But I failed and Oh dear! I was in trouble from my mother.

I used to ride in all those beastly shows, and the minute the class was over, I was put in the horse-box and sent home. That was it. Whereas in this day and age, all the kids ride in the show-ring, and then off they go and meet each other and go on to the fair, and all have a jolly-up together. There was none of that. It wasn't because it was the fashion in those days: it was because of my mother, who definitely wanted to keep me to herself. That was the answer.

She was a very strong character indeed. She was the only character in my life that I got to know frightfully well who was always intimidating. I don't think she intimidated other people.

9

Standing with some of the trophies I had won that season. These ponies were always produced by my mother who was not only a wonderful judge, but also excelled at producing first-class show horses.

And I don't know why she frightened me. But she did. Always.

My brother Crosby, who was four years older than me, is still alive. I don't think my mother intimidated him nearly so much. He was lucky: he was sent away to boarding school. So he mixed with other people like you do when you're away at school. He led an entirely different life. Whereas I was clamped at home to do nothing but ride the ponies and take them to the shows, and as soon as they were any good, they were sold. And then I had to start on another one. The same thing applied to the show horses and hunters. They were there to be made a living out of, and I was the means to that end. It was very much a business.

Crosby rode, and he rode in point-to-points, whereas he wouldn't have the show-ring, which is why he escaped my mother. He rode and hunted all his life, and only gave up hunting at Christmas 1988, aged seventy-four, a great character, and a member of the Warwickshire Hunt Committee for forty years. He rode some point-to-point winners and he's kept point-to-point winners, and sold a horse he bred called Thursby to Anne,

10

Duchess of Westminster in the summer of '89. He also bred Rough House who won the SGB chase and Great Yorkshire at Doncaster trained by us.

I don't think I was particularly strict with my own children: they had an entirely different upbringing. But when they were small, Fred and I were working frightfully hard because we had got to make our own living. So possibly we didn't spend as much time with our children as we should have done. We were too busy earning our living. And that was racing: we knew no other way. We started literally from scratch. We had got to do it. If I lived my life over again I would say that we didn't spend as much time with our children as we should have done. On the other hand, I don't think they were spoilt and they had a good life. I don't approve of the way that lots of children are brought up in this day and age. In my day children were supposed to be seen and not heard, and I think many of them could do with that today. And they should be put to bed at the proper time.

I could ride for as long as I can remember, and by the time I was

This photograph was taken of me at an Oxfordshire show when I was about 10. On the left is Beryl, daughter of that great judge of steeple-chasers Harry Bonner – he used to buy old Lord Bicester's famous horses.

11

ten years old, I did a tremendous lot of riding in the show-ring. As soon as my mother got a good show pony and won a few times, it was sold. So I had to embark on another one. Consequently I never reaped the benefit of having a very good pony being kept for me; it was always passed on. The ponies were a money-making project, so therefore I was making ponies and producing them from the age of nine.

When I was ten I was selected to ride for England in France and I went over with my pony with a team organised by Cecil Aldin, the artist. It's a commonplace thing today for children to ride abroad, but in those days it was quite unique – eight or nine children to be despatched to France to ride against the French. I won on the pony at Le Touquet, and the then Prince of Wales, afterwards Edward VIII, presented me with my cup. Whilst I was there, unbeknown to me, a Spanish princess, Princess Hohenloe, saw the pony and decided she would like to buy it for her family. When we came back this beautiful pony called The Sheikh was sold and went out to Spain. This was just before the Spanish Civil War, and when the family had had it for just under a year, they wrote to mother and asked, 'Would Mercy go out and ride it for them, because we can't ride it.'

So my mother and I went out. The aristocracy weren't very popular under their Communist government, and my mother didn't realise that telephones and telegrams and things didn't work quite like they did in England. We were told to get off the train at Escorial. We got off at this small station, there was nobody to meet us and my mother couldn't speak a word of Spanish. Except for that trip to France the year before, we had never been abroad before. All my mother had got was the address on the notepaper heading. She showed it to some men near the station and that wasn't frightfully popular. A man with a black beret, in a leather jacket, suggested we get into his car and we set off. My mother was obviously terrified because we drove for two hours right through the hills, and rugged wild country, full of boulders. She thought we were being kidnapped or something, and taken to somewhere awful. Eventually we came to an enormous portcullis gate, like you see in films. The man blew the horn and the gate opened and in we went and she turned to me and she said 'We've been taken to a monastery or a convent.' But it proved to be the Princess's castle and they were all apologetic because they hadn't received the cable we'd sent.

Hunting with the Warwickshire aged 14 on one of the good show ponies which was purchased by my mother from Charlie Edwards. The previous year it had been shown at the Royal Show and Charlie Edwards had entered a bay pony. The bay pony went lame but, determined to show a pony, he dyed this grey pony with permanganate of potash. Lady Hunloke, who was judging, said, 'That's the most lovely pony but it's an extraordinary colour! I can't put it up.' My mother saw it, subsequently purchased it, and it was a great success for me, winning everywhere the following season.

We were looked after magnificently. Strangely enough one of the brothers of the Spanish family, who's a bit younger than me, is Prince Alfonso, who started the Club at Marbella. We stayed with them for a couple of weeks and then returned home – no aeroplanes – by train.

Thirty years later Fred and I were in Marbella, staying at the Marbella Club and playing tennis, when Fred did something to his ankle. He went into the bar and Alfonso walked in. So Fred said laughingly, 'I think you know my wife,' and he said, 'What was her name?' and so Fred said, 'Mercy Cockburn.' 'Oh yes,' he said, 'She's the first little girl I ever saw in jodhpurs,' and with that out he came and entertained us, and was absolutely marvellous. I met him again three or four years ago, when I was in the Marbella Club. having a meal, and he still recognised me, which I thought was extraordinary.

By the time I'd reached the age of thirteen I was looking for something more exciting than showing ponies. The natural progress was into racing. So I decided I'd ride in point-to-points. I rode my first winner when I was fourteen, which wouldn't be allowed today, but in those days you could ride at any age. Naturally I can remember the horse's name: it was called Leicester Square. Point-to-pointing gave me a marvellous thrill. And it started me off in racing. Two years later I met Fred at a tennis party in June, so I was just sixteen. He was my only boyfriend. I've always been what you'd call a one-man woman and I didn't really ever have any other boyfriends, and I was married when I was seventeen.

It was a bit of an odd life. In those days Fred was a leading jockey and in 1938–39 he was Champion Jockey for the first time with sixty-one winners, following his brother-in-law, Gerry Wilson, who'd been Champion six years running since 1932, but he'd only once ridden as many as sixty-one winners. From then my life became completely racing-orientated and it has been ever since.

Then came the war and things were hard. Fred drove those awful 'Queen Mary' lorries in the RAF – there was no racing for part of the war so I decided I'd revert to my old habits. I started to buy some ponies to make some money out of selling them, which was the only thing I knew about. So I had to start and deal in something I knew about, which I did quite successfully. Even in the middle of the war there were all sorts of people wanting ponies and show ponies. Therefore I was virtually financing the household.

During the war Ida Croxon, a very famous point-to-point rider, lived with us in Church House, Severn Stoke. She had hairs where a moustache would be and I decided they should be removed. So I bought some Elizabeth Arden wax, and Fred held her on the kitchen table, while I pulled the wax off. She then had a white streak along her upper lip, and chased us both with a carving knife!

I had no means of transport in those days, so I bought myself a scooter. That wasn't very good because it was too slow. I got a pony and trap which was even slower. So then I bought myself a Norton 500 c.c. motor bike and that was very successful. I only had a very small petrol allowance but I eked it out with the motor bike.

Guy was born just before the war, and the one thing I clung onto was the nanny. I was determined to keep her even if I scrubbed the floors and did everything else, so he would be looked after and I could get about. Which I did. I also took in paying guests.

When the war finished Fred started riding again. It was difficult because he had put on weight. However, he soon got back up to the top again, splitting the title with 'Frenchie' Nicholson in 1944–45 and winning again in 1945–46.

In the early days Fred used to go down with Doug Francis (Dick's elder brother) to Devon in August and I used to stay behind to take my daughter Scarlett to the local shows. They always joked that Connie Poole, who also lived with us, was the

Fred, aged 12, with his first winner – you could ride that young in those days. The horse, Rolie, owned by his grandfather and trained by his father, won at Chepstow.

15

spy to see that Fred behaved himself. At a dance down there, Connie tripped over a cable and put out all the lights. 'That's polished off the spy!' said Doug.

Then we had a nasty setback: Fred broke his neck on a horse called Poet Prince of Fulke Walwyn's at Wincanton. It was three weeks before the Gold Cup and he would have ridden it at Cheltenham. Fred started riding again nine months later, but the following March (1947) he broke his back again in the Gold Cup on Coloured School Boy. He never rode again.

When he broke his neck the first time at Wincanton, I drove him back from the course. You wouldn't be allowed to do that now, but I went into the ambulance room. He asked them to go out and get him a cup of tea. Whilst they were getting a cup of tea, somehow or other I got him into some clothes, a coat and got him into the car because he didn't want to go to Wincanton Cottage Hospital. I'm not casting any aspersions at the Cottage Hospital, but the one thought in our minds was to get him back to his own doctor in Cheltenham. It was a mad thing to do; in hindsight it shouldn't have been done. Anyway, I got him home, I don't know how and into the hospital next day, and then of course they were horrified. They X-rayed him and they found his neck had broken right up at the third and fourth vertebrae. After all that drama they then plonked him into the most horrible plaster, which went over his head and down to his waist and he had to stick in that for three months.

We went to St Thomas's Hospital in London, to Dr Perkins, and he said 'I'll take it off as long as you promise not to trip up some steps or do anything stupid.' So he cut this wretched plaster cast off. Fred's hair by that time was hanging over his shoulders, so he said 'The first thing I'm going to do is to walk over the bridge and find a hairdresser and have my hair washed. I don't want to come with you in the taxi.' And walking across the bridge over the Thames, Fred, of course, tripped up!

That was when he put on all his weight because he was confined in his beastly plaster cast for three months. I realised after the second break that it was going to be the same thing all over again. I knew all the symptoms. I'm an authority on hospitals. I've been in and out of them with all these jockeys over the years.

Someone said that 'Fred was lucky to survive – walking about with a broken neck.' But he didn't walk back. He got into the car,

Fred's father leading Forbra after training him to win the 1932 Grand National ridden by Tim Hamey. Tim Hamey, father of Rex, is now the oldest surviving jockey to have won the Grand National.

in those days we had a big old Packard, and I got him home. We laid him on the back seat for a journey I'll never forget. It was the most horrendous journey: he was sick all the time.

The second time he did it at Cheltenham I knew what had happened to him. They took him straight to hospital and the doctor was somebody we knew very well. He's dead now, he was a super doctor, but he used to get on the bottle. Fred was lying on the hospital bed when the doctor said we must pull Fred's boots off. I looked across at the sister, and she looked across at me. I made a sign to her and she knew what I meant, so I said to her 'Why don't *you* cut them off?' She did. Obviously, he was jolly lucky, because he was paralysed for a bit and wore a plastic collar. Anyway, all was well in the end.

I suppose that until Fred died I'd never stood on my own feet before. How could I, married at seventeen? My life had revolved around Fred. And although everybody thinks that I probably made the major decisions, I didn't. He made them. It was a case of good understanding. No major decision about anything in life, was ever reached without him. He had all the say, well, most of it anyway. He was nearly always right. He was a much better judge of what was right and what was wrong than I was. He was a much wiser person than me, in every respect, I would say. And I say that because I respected him.

As a judge of character, I think I was possibly as good as he was. He was a much better mixer than me, much more the *bon viveur* type of person. He could talk to anybody about almost anything, he didn't see anything bad in anybody, ever, but always picked out the good. I am obviously biased, but I think he was a tremendous character in every way, really. He certainly did lots of good things in his life. I wasn't such a good mixer, because I was shyer. Fundamentally I have always been a shy person and a bit of a loner which was the way I was brought up. Whereas he was brought up in a much more open, gregarious way of life, in the racing world. Racing makes you a better mixer, because you have to get on with people. Even after I'd married him, I still found it quite hard to talk to people because I had never been allowed to mix with people before.

What attracted me about Fred all those years ago was that he'd got great charisma – I think that's the word you'd use now – and he was very good-looking, as the photographs bear out. I was young and impressionable and I do think we sort of fell in love, if

This lovely old photograph of Kinnersley was taken in the early 1930s. Fred is standing in the centre with his father on his right.

you like to call it that. He had great sympathy for an animal, it didn't matter what it was: a horse, a dog or a beast. He had great animal understanding. That's something you're born with. It's a thing you can't learn. You either have an instinctive feeling for animals or you don't. I have five grandchildren and, funnily enough, I have only one with what I call 'animal sense' and he doesn't even ride.

Fred was the most amusing person, a wonderful raconteur and very athletic. He was keen on all sorts of sports: tennis, cricket and racing and he loved hunting and so did I. I'd been brought up all

Fred and me, taken on holiday at Sandbanks when I was 16 and Fred was Champion Jockey shortly before we were engaged.

my life to hunt. Fred loved all country pursuits the same as I did. We liked the same things. And that is essential if you are going to make a go of married life. You've really got to have the same tastes. We were married for forty-four years, and that's a long time, especially in the world we lived in, for the racing world isn't noted for its lengthy liaisons.

It would have been very nice indeed, if there had been someone in the family to follow on as a trainer, after nearly seventy years of Rimells here, but unfortunately it wasn't to be. I suppose Guy had racing rammed down his throat from the time he could remember, and he just rebelled, like people do rebel. He did ride a hunter 'chase winner and several point-to-point winners, so he was a capable rider. At 6'3", he obviously hadn't got the build to be a rider, so it was always out of the question that he'd be a jockey. It was just nice that he was able to ride that hunter 'chase winner, on a horse my father bred and gave Guy as a gift.

But now Guy doesn't have anything to do with racing at all; he has no interest in it. He was never really in racing properly and he simply drifted out. His marriage went wrong. That was the end of his having anything to do with what I call our sort of life and he went to live abroad. He's lived abroad now for twelve years in Marbella, dealing in power boats.

He's always been keen on boats, goodness knows why. He sells boats in Spain and has been very successful at it. He's done it all on his own with no assistance from anybody. He built himself two houses and sold them, and in 1989 he built another one.

We never envisaged him coming into racing, because you have to have a certain sort of personality to be in racing, and Guy just wasn't racing-orientated. Whereas Scarlett, my daughter, is completely different, and was racing-orientated from the word go. Had she been the boy and Guy the girl, it would have been completely different. Scarlett still loves racing.

Guy is the father of Katie the owner and rider of Three Counties. He has three children, but the only who has inherited the love of racing is Katie. There are two brothers, and the one brother hates horses and hates racing and has nothing to do with it. The other one rides extremely well and was short-listed for the Junior European event team. He's a very good event rider at only 18. But he's not racing-minded.

Scarlett won the Newmarket Town Plate when she was aged fourteen, which you can imagine was an enormous thrill. We got her out of school to ride and I think she was the youngest person ever to have won it.

She couldn't wait to ride point-to-pointing. The first horse she had was a little Vulgan mare which I bought unseen, an extraordinary thing to do, in Ireland off Cyril Bryce-Smith. I sent Professor Martin Byrne to vet it, and said 'If it's absolutely awful, spin it, and if it's all right, pass it!' Martin rang up and said, 'You'll love it.' She was the last horse we ever had that arrived by rail, at Defford station, and she came via Holyhead and then by train.

Scarlett was an excellent rider. She won 14 point-to-points on her and lots of other races too. And then when she got married she didn't ride point-to-pointing any more, which possibly was a good thing.

Robin Knipe hadn't got the stud when they married. In those days he had a herd of milking cows. That was a bind, and at that time the government were paying you to go out of milking, so he took the payment, and decided he would take a chance and set up the stud the other side of Hereford at Cobhall Court. Fred and I went to Newmarket with him, and between us we bought Celtic Cone. It's been a success story because they've gone into it very professionally. Both of them are frightfully interested, and very horse minded, and they have made an enormous success of their stud. Any money they've made, they've ploughed back into their own place. It's really first-class.

Robin had been a very good rider, too. He was a leading amateur one year, and then unfortunately broke his back at Warwick in a hunter 'chase. He spent six months in Stoke Mandeville, so that was another trauma we had to live through, for it looked as if he wouldn't ever walk again. They have two children, one not really horse-inclined: a boy who doesn't ride at all, and a girl, Tracey, who was very successful in the show ring riding side-saddle. She carried on the family tradition by winning her side-saddle class two years running at the Royal Show.

We were married at St Mary's Church, Warwick, only a short distance from Castle Lane where I used to gallop my pony and visit the blacksmith on days I was meant to be in school.

Scarlett never contemplated going into training at Kinnersley. They have their own place and their own stud business which is completely different to training, and they're very successful. They wouldn't have come to Kinnersley anyway, because they would never have gone to a rented place which means, as with me, that you've no final say in staying or going. They're happier doing what they're doing, and they do it very well. Scarlett's very knowledgeable about racing.

22

There was no question of my making Scarlett ride against her will – if anything it was preventing her! No, Scarlett loved it and fortunately Robin is the same and now they can afford to have a horse in training as well. They've had the odd horse or two over the years and most of them have been successful. They are still frightfully keen on racing, which has been marvellous for me since Fred died, because Scarlett or Robin have often come racing with me, which has been a tremendous help, and great company. But they do live an hour away from me and they have their own lives to live.

Guy, my son, has three children, the eldest of whom is Katie, who has been so successful with Three Counties. She lived with me for three years, that's a bonus to have a grand-daughter living with you, especially one that was mad keen on riding.

The horse we were lucky enough to buy for her, Three Counties, has been unique. He has won the Horse and Hound Cup two years running and he was twice second in the Foxhunters at Cheltenham and then went on to win it. It's what you call 'A grandmothers' horse', because it was paid for her by her grandmother Lyons (whose husband Sir William had been head of Jaguar) and given to her as a twenty-first birthday present. And *I* found the horse and did the buying and training. I was staying with Michael Purcell in Tipperary. He knew what I wanted and he had seen the horse running. It had won one novice 'chase. He thought that it would be an ideal contestant for the job. We went and saw it and bought it in the field without ever having it ridden.

Katie had ridden in the show ring, and hunter trials and a few odd events, from day one. She had always been keen on horses and had always ridden.

Three Counties won the Christies' Foxhunters at Cheltenham in 1989, my last winner as a trainer, and he would have won the year before too, if Fred Winter hadn't run Observe. It annoyed me intensely that you had got a horse that was well backed and had run in the previous Gold Cup, then to see it switched round and run in the Foxhunters. Fred Winter was quite correct in doing so. The rules are the rules and he abided by them. He ran his horse and I can't blame him. I just think it is a wrong rule. A hunter chaser should not be allowed to run in a hunter chase if it has won a race worth £2000 during the two previous seasons.

On Stewards 2

I don't think the standard of *local* stewarding has improved, but you're much better to have bungling amateurs than crooked professionals. Certainly the *stipendiary* stewards today are far better qualified than they used to be. They all go to seminars and therefore they are trained. They guide the local stewards. By and large, I think the stewarding is very good. I always have done. It's perfectly fair. Any time I've been in front of them the enquiries have been fair and correctly conducted. I have no argument with them. We're all human, we all make errors. The stewards have got a pretty thankless task. They are always open to be shot at, and there are always the people in the stands who think they know more than somebody who, in this day and age, has got the opportunity to see the videos, in slow motion, head on and side on.

Overall we're far better with the class and the type of steward that we have than if we employed all professional stewards. I'm against professional stewards. They have got the one professional stipendiary steward, and though he's there to guide them, they should reach their own decision. But the 'stipe' is there as a guide.

But they could make more use of people who've had active racing experience such as Dick Saunders, Tim Holland-Martin, that type of person, who have had a lot of practical experience in race-riding. Those sort of people must know more than the ex-army man or the retired businessman who's worked in an office all his life and now, just because he's got nothing to do or was in the army, they incorporate him and make him a steward. That's wrong. They don't know anything about riding.

People who've had point-to-pointing or race-riding experience might be thin on the ground, but I would have thought you could have found enough. For instance, my son-in-law, Robin Knipe – I quote him only because I just happen to know – you would have thought they would have made him a steward at his local courses like Hereford and Worcester. He was a leading amateur before he broke his back and he's got no axe to grind because he now runs a stud. That type of person, and there are lots of others.

But they don't ask them. The asking is done by the Clerk of the Course. He has to find the stewards for his track. The 'stipes' are allotted by Weatherbys. They have to cover so many courses per week, and by and large, they are very good. But the local stewards are gathered up together by the Clerk of the Course often for social reasons.

The 'stipes' are better now in that they know about it. When you've got the videos, it makes life so much easier. I don't know whether it's better for the jockeys or not! It's easier for the stewards. It's much easier, using the videos, to stop non-triers. They can do them in slow motion and they can do a 'stop' on them. You can really see absolutely everything.

There are less non-triers jumping than there were. In the old days people would lay horses out for the big handicaps like the Schweppes. But today stake money has gone up, and as it's very expensive to keep a horse in training, you've got to try and win what you can. I don't think there are quite the big gambles that there used to be – possibly there are in flat racing, but I don't think there are in jumping.

Perhaps because jumping has a different type of owner, or perhaps people haven't got the patience. If now you can win three races during a season, hopefully you will virtually pay the horse's keep. If you can pay your horse's keep when all is said and done, it is still a sport, whereas flat racing is a business. So if you can pay a horse's keep for the twelve months in stake money, you are getting your fun for nothing.

I'm told at certain golf courses you have to pay five hundred quid for two or three games of golf. That's an expensive sport and you've *no* return. The same with yachting or motor-racing. You've no return whatsoever. In racing you have got a *hope* of some return.

Neither Fred nor I laid out horses for handicaps. It really wasn't our style. Everybody has a different style of racing and that just wasn't ours, although we did manage to win the big handicap at Haydock which started as the Royal Doulton, and was the most valuable handicap hurdle in the Calendar, even more valuable than the Schweppes. We managed to win that with Royal Gaye

and Gaye Chance – and then I was second in it with Gala's Image. But they were all exposed horses.

Ryan Price laid himself out to win the Schweppes: there's no doubt about it and he was very successful at it. He always said he didn't gamble but somebody must have gambled, so whether it was him or whether it was his owners, I can't tell. With the video and a better type of 'stipe' it's much harder to cheat with horses. The only chance you've probably got of getting a horse handicapped in a race like that today is to have a good novice and win one pretty poor novice hurdle, and then put it in a big handicap. Then you've done nothing wrong and yet you're handicapped.

Fred riding Forbra at Newbury after he had won the National. The jockey on the right is Danny Morgan who later trained Roddy Owen to win the 1959 Cheltenham Gold Cup.

27

Fred going down to the start of the National on Avenger, the favourite. Going out into the country for the second time he fell at the first fence and broke his neck.

At the smaller courses the professional steward dominates the amateurs, but at your bigger meetings where you've got very, very well-qualified amateurs, then they do as they think, and just take guidance from the 'stipe'.

Some jockeys would make very good stewards, and on the other hand some of them would make bad ones. You would have to sift the wheat from the chaff. Richard Linley, for instance, now an Inspector of Courses, would have made an excellent steward. He's level-headed and he knows what he's talking about. That type would have been the right calibre for a steward.

I didn't have the misfortune to be called in front of the stewards many times. It's nothing like it used to be. On the few odd occasions when I have had to go in they've always been perfectly polite. You're ushered into a smallish room, and the chairman, the senior steward of the meeting, is sitting in the chair in the middle. He has one steward on one side and another steward on the other, and the stipendiary steward is standing. They do offer you a chair now to sit down. Then you're shown a video. They will ask you the relevant questions and then ask you to go outside. They call you back in when they've held their own private discussion. If they've had occasion to have the jockey in as well, he'll sometimes go in with you, depending what it's over, or sometimes separately. Then you go back in and you know your sentence. They either accept your explanation or they say, 'Well, I'm sorry, but we shall fine you the statutory fine.' In the olden days it was very autocratic, and on some occasions probably not correct, but today there isn't much wrong with it.

They had me in at Worcester over Gaye Chance which I couldn't quite understand. He hadn't run frightfully well – I don't quite know why – he just had an off day and was second. Horses aren't machines, they do have off days. The stipendiary steward came and said 'The stewards would like to see you and will you make yourself available'. I wasn't nervous: I had nothing to be nervous about. I was slightly apprehensive. And slightly worried about the way my horse had run. In my heart I thought they really were entitled to ask me. The only assumption I could draw was that he might have got a bit of a virus. I didn't run him again for about six weeks, and by the time he ran again he was perfectly all right. When we got him home, we didn't find anything wrong with him.

The 'stipe' showed me in and I sat down faced with three men. The chairman of the committee of three showed me a video of the race and asked the questions. He said 'Can you explain your horse's running, Mrs Rimell?'

I said, 'No, as a matter of fact, I can't.'

'Because', they said, 'we think that he ran a little below his form. Your horse was a very short-price favourite and he's got beaten.'

And I said, 'Yes, he has. Well, he never got to the winner, Migrator, who jumped off and made all, and was a very fit horse. It had run already. It was my horse's first run of the season – and the other was fit. The only assumption I can come to is that my horse probably wasn't quite as ready as I thought he was, and the other horse just got first run on him – he was never able to get to him.'

The two other stewards didn't ask me any questions. And then I was told to go out while they considered my case. Then after about five minutes waiting in the weighing room, I was invited back in and they said 'We accept your explanation.' They put the verdict on a pink slip and it is put outside in a little case. They put the photo-finishes up and they put the stewards' findings up as well. They used not to do that but they do now.

I have been had in once or twice over an apprentice who had probably ridden a bit of an injudicious finish. One dropped his hands at Wincanton and something came up and caught him on the post for second place. You have to go in then because you are answerable for how your apprentice behaves. But the stewards were very fair. All they did was give him a caution which he fully deserved.

He most certainly should have finished second, and I was pleased when they had him in and that they had me in with him. I was answerable for his actions because he was apprenticed to me. When they showed me the video I was horrified! They asked me how long he had been with me and how many rides had he had. They could look it up quite easily, but it saves them the bother. I told them to the best of my ability and they said 'What do you think?' and I said 'I quite agree. He did ride a stupid race, he dropped his hands and he should have been second.' And as it was his first offence, they were very fair and didn't fine him, but it would have served him right had they done so. They cautioned him, very correctly.

On the whole, local stewarding is pretty good. Everybody seems to forget that the punters are obviously speaking through their pockets. We are all human beings and we all make errors. The stewards do drop a clanger every now and again, but don't we all? Press men love to fasten onto something that is horrid. If something good has happened they never report it. If something absolutely vile has happened, they can't wait to splash it across the headlines.

I've never been before the stewards in London. I have never committed such a serious crime.

3 *On Jockeys*

Jockeys ride different types of races now than they used to. These last seasons you've seen Peter Scudamore riding a tremendous lot of races from the front. He's made the running on most of the winners he's had. Whether those are his instructions or not I can't tell, but he's ridden more races from the front than you've seen any other champion jockey ride.

Fred Winter's great strength was his *strength*! He was a very good jockey but –comparisons are odious anyway – he never struck me as being quite the best I've known. John Francome was a very good rider. I found almost every jockey who rode for us honest, and helpful. We never gave them detailed orders. Terry Biddlecombe never had an order in his life. Peter Scudamore rode quite a lot of winners for me over the years, and I don't think I ever gave him any orders. I always got on with him frightfully well.

You say to them, 'This horse always likes to be up there,' or 'This horse wants dropping out: give him a chance and he'll find a fair bit of speed at the finish,' something like that. You don't tie down a good jockey. That's what you pay a jockey for: for him to use his head. You either say 'He stays very well and you can make plenty of use of him,' or 'He barely gets the trip.' You don't tie them down with a million orders. At least I didn't and Fred never did.

Richard Linley I liked very much, and he was a very good horseman, and intelligent. The four years he rode for me were very satisfactory, both for him, for me and for Sheikh Ali. The whole thing was a satisfactory partnership. I suppose one could have said that perhaps Richard wasn't the most forceful jockey in the world, and one always used to think that perhaps he just didn't quite ride a horse into the last as well as he might have done. But he seemed to get results. And he was a good horseman:

he gave a horse a beautiful ride in a race. And the whole thing, as far as I was concerned, worked very well.

Sam Morshead was a bit wild. He would be apt to get horses unbalanced, and he wasn't one of our best jockeys by any means. He was a very brave jockey, too brave perhaps for he got horses a bit unbalanced.

John Burke, the son of a schoolmaster in County Meath, was a much better rider. He would be in a different league altogether. He was a very good rider, a very good horseman, and won a lot of big races for us. He was excellent. And being very light, he never had any problems with weight. We didn't part with Burke. He parted with us. He had a problem. So he left us.

He succeeded Ken White, who was a very good rider. Ken won a Champion Hurdle for us, but he lacked the flair that Terry Biddlecombe had. He was a very adequate rider. Possibly he had been going round a long time, and ridden a lot of bad horses before he started to ride our good horses. One always thought he was the old nagsman type of rider. But there was nothing wrong with Ken. He could do a very light weight. He was a very nice person and a very sympathetic rider, who would never knock a horse about, the same as John Burke would never knock a horse about.

Then before that there was Terry who had all the flair in the world, all the charisma, and I am sure won more races for us that he shouldn't have won, than the races that he lost. I can't say much higher than that. Terry's weakness was his weight and his lifestyle. Sometimes, I think, he didn't go to sleep much the night before a race!

Tim Vinall was a very quiet unobtrusive little man and rode his horses in that quiet manner. I never thought he was quite forceful enough, but he was very sympathetic and rode horses the way he was himself. In no way was he a flamboyant character like Terry Biddlecombe.

Very often, the way jockeys ride is an expression of their characters. Terry was very flamboyant, and a very, very good rider. In his heyday he was a terrific jockey. He had courage and balance – these were his main assets. In his early years his riding ability was excellent. He'd been brought up in the gymkhana world, for his father was king of the gymkhanas round here. His great downfall was the fact that he was a playboy.

Once we went to Norway to run Robert Sangster's Sunny Lad in

Fred winning the Champion Hurdle on Brain's Trust. Davy Jones is second, Don Butchers is third and Tommy Farmer on the wide outside was fourth. Brain's Trust was trained by Gerry Wilson, Fred's brother-in-law.

the Norwegian Grand National, and flew over to Oslo in one of the Sangster planes. The Norwegians entertained us very well so the night before the race we decided to lock Terry in his bedroom. Chris Sangster, Robert's first wife, even put a chair under the door handle to jam it so he couldn't possibly escape. But Terry was very resourceful. We went back to check half an hour later and he'd gone. He had escaped through the window, crawled along the window sill, and climbed into another room. God knows when he returned! He probably stayed out all night. Sunny Lad finished third. Possibly he ought to have won for he carried 6lb or 8lb overweight, due to the excesses of the previous night . . .

Terry was amazing. He could get away with murder. On the mornings he came to ride out, he'd walk into the yard at one minute to eight. Fred always said Terry simply didn't know how to make a horse ready or how to put a set of tack on one. He'd just get on a horse and that was it. When he got injured, Fred would ask him to come over and work in the yard for a bit to find out how it all was done. But he never came.

One Boxing Day we had two runners: Charlie Lad of Crawford Scott's (and later that season sold to Sybil Joseph) and Impact, a little grey. I was despatched to Newton Abbot with them and I drove down with Terry, who had obviously had a night out. All the way down he moaned, groaned and grumbled or slept as I drove. It was snowing and I kept thinking, 'We'll get there, and it'll be abandoned'.

We thought both horses would win and both owners liked a bet. When we got into the paddock for the first race it was snowing, and Terry looked very sour. I said to him: 'You *will* win and make *no* mistake about it! Out of the gate and always up there!' He did. He came out to ride the grey and I said, 'This'll win easier.' It did. So coming back Terry was all smiles – 'I'll drive,' he said. That was Terry all over – up one minute, down the next.

At his best, there was no better rider. He was a tremendous opportunist. His good races far outnumbered the few duff ones. He should have won a second National on Gay Trip in '72. That was *not* one of his better efforts. Stuck on the outside all the way

*Fred's father with, on
the right, Sir Edward
Hanmer, who was our
longest-standing owner
and for whom we won
the Gold Cup, just before
he died.*

round and then beaten two lengths, when he must have given away thirty! And we were giving 22lb to the winner Well To Do. Impossible. But Terry made fewer mistakes than most and won a lot of races others wouldn't have done.

Fearless Fred was a desperate jumper, but won twenty-one races. Terry used to ride him and I don't know how he survived on him.

Bill Smith was Terry's exact opposite. I never got on with him ever – as a man or a jockey. But he won us a Champion Hurdle and a Triumph Hurdle. Terry was a complete extrovert; Bill Smith was absolutely the reverse. We never saw eye to eye. I'd got used to the open, Biddlecombe way. Terry would always say what he thought and you could have fun with him. You couldn't with Bill Smith. He didn't do anything wrong, so far as I can recall, when he was riding for us. But his character just didn't fit. When he left it was a perfectly amicable end to the relationship. He'd got friendly with the Walwyns and they offered him a retainer. He told Fred about it and said 'I'd like to accept.'

But I don't think Fred was sorry to see him go. We'd got used to Terry and he was a very hard act to follow. After eight or nine years you build a close association with your rider. We had a lot of horses in those days and you see an awful lot of your jockey. You want to respect them and be friendly with them as well as admiring their ability.

Ken White had more sympathy for a horse than any other of our riders. For him a horse wasn't just a machine, a means to an end. He'd always been around, riding second to Terry and had ridden a lot of winners for us. Comedy's second Champion Hurdle in 1975 and a Mackeson Gold Cup on Chatham in 1970, for instance, when Terry couldn't do the weight of 10st 3lb. It was an automatic transition – I don't know how we got carried away with Bill Smith!

Ken managed Comedy very well. Ken was so light he could do 9st 8lb, and Comedy was a massive horse, but he got on wonderfully well with him. I was always terribly pleased that Ken did in the end ride a Champion Hurdle winner, because he'd always rather been 'second' in all ways. It was very rewarding for everybody that he rode him when he won.

John Burke followed Ken White, and he was certainly the second best jockey we ever had: Terry was the best with John Burke running a close second. John Burke came to us from Ireland when he was seventeen to ride as an amateur. He rode in some

My mother and a friend at the Horse and Hound *Ball in the early 1950s.*

point-to-points and then gradually progressed to riding under rules. Of all the riders we ever had over the years, he was the best horseman. Terry was the best jockey, but John Burke was the best horseman. He'd got great sympathy for a horse and the most beautiful hands.

Nobody but he would have won the Grand National on Rag Trade. Rag Trade was such a poor jumper, that after John Francome rode him the year before, he said 'That's the most horrible horse I've ever ridden, and I'll never ride him again in anything.' John Francome was a very, very good jockey, so that says a lot for John Burke.

He was a very nice quiet Irishman. Unfortunately for him he had a lot of success when he was very young. He was only twenty-one when he won the National and the Gold Cup in the same year 1976 and two years later in 1978 he won the Triumph Hurdle for us on Connaught Ranger. Those victories so early went to his head, I'm afraid, and he had a bit of a problem with the drinking. He disappeared out of the game. A marvellous horseman, but he lost his way. Too much success too soon, and he wasn't mentally quite ready for it.

I wouldn't say Bobby Beasley was a good horseman, but he was a very good jockey. He was very temperamental, and got frightfully depressed. If things weren't going well, he was terribly pessimistic. He was never what you'd call a very cheery soul, but he rode a tremendous lot of winners – not so many for us, because the season he came and rode for us we didn't have a very good season.

Bobby Beasley didn't really want to ride Nicolaus Silver in the National, he wanted to ride some Irish horse in the race. But we'd engaged him and we said 'No, you've got to stick.' And that was it. Anyway he won the National, but he was difficult, and so temperamental that he took far more controlling than any of our owners!

At that time we had badly wanted Stan Mellor as stable jockey. But he took too long thinking about the offer, so that by the time he had made up his mind and rang up to say, 'Yes, I'll take the job,' we had already gone and engaged Beasley. Fred being Fred wouldn't go back on his word. It was most unfortunate, because we got on very well with Stan and it would, I'm sure, have been a much happier relationship.

Fred had asked Stan a month beforehand, and he'd been sort of thinking about it. So Fred said, 'I really want to know, because several of our owners are asking, "Well, who's going to be our jockey?"' So Fred asked Beasley and he said, 'Yes.' Then that very night – it was just one of those flukes of life – Stan rang up and said yes, he would do it. Though Fred felt he couldn't go back on his word, in hindsight, it would have been much better if he had.

If you go back to the Dave Dick days, modern jockeys ride by comparison, very much shorter. You see a picture of Dave Dick riding E.S.B. when he won the 1956 National for us, and he's riding almost hunting length. My memory of somebody riding really short in the National was Andrew Turnell. He must have had wonderful balance because he was a good rider, but yet rode terrifically short. Good jockeys find the length at which they feel comfortable, and they ride it. Today you've got a good rider in Tom Morgan, who rides quite long compared with some of the other jockeys you see.

But Francome didn't ride frightfully short. It's awfully difficult to compare jockeys. Obviously Francome was a very, very good rider. He wasn't my jockey, though he rode the odd winner or two for me. He was principally Fred Winter's jockey, and maybe

My mother on Thomastown, one of her show horses, outside her home at Barford in the late '50s.

it's because he's more recent that he stands out as a very, very good rider.

Of all the jockeys I've seen, I suppose I would have taken Francome as the best. He's a very good horseman and he's intelligent. Peter Scudamore's a good rider, but I don't think he's yet the most stylish. But he certainly gets results. The standard now is as high as it's been for years. Scudamore sets a very good example and not just as a jockey. He's got beautiful manners, he dresses neatly and he doesn't let his hair fall over his shoulders. As a rider I tend to put him into the Biddlecombe bracket, because he thumps a bit on the back of the saddle. Terry wasn't the most stylish rider in the world, but he certainly got results. That wonderful balance of Terry's was half the secret of his success.

It's very nice to have a jockey intelligent and articulate enough to tell you something after a race. Funnily enough, the jockey who used to be the best at telling us about a horse was Tim Brookshaw, who rode for us for quite a few seasons. He wasn't a very stylish rider, but he got results. He was certainly very intelligent. He

40

My father at a race meeting, in the 1950s talking to Connie Poole, still a great friend of mine who lived with us during the War and used to 'chaperone' Fred in the West Country . . .

could not only tell you about the horse he'd ridden, but about most of the others in the race, and that's always quite handy to know. Poor Tim: a terrible end to his life.

At the end I hadn't sufficient horses to retain a jockey. There's no point in paying somebody a huge retainer when you haven't got the number of horses to afford it.

Hopefully there are quite a lot of good boys coming on. But it's very difficult to get a boy going unless you've got a big yard with a lot of horses. Then you're in a position really to be very much in command. You can say to an owner, 'I want to put a boy up on this horse. I think it would be a good idea to take seven pounds off his back, and this boy's a good boy,' and all that sort of thing. Big trainers are able to do that, whereas smaller trainers aren't. You know what owners are: they always want to have the leading jockey. They think that if you have a top jockey he'll make the horse win, regardless of whether the horse is good enough or not.

Of course, if a jockey's riding winners, he's riding with a lot of confidence, he'll reach a decision during the race when he knows

41

he's got to be in a certain position to have any chance of winning. He'll take that split-second decision, whereas a jockey that hasn't had the experience or is out of form doesn't realise so quickly. If he had, then he'd have had a better chance.

I still don't approve of women jockeys – except in point-to-points and hunter 'chases, of course. Really, they're not the right make or shape for it.

The conditional jockeys' system is quite wrong at the moment. It shouldn't be limited by age. Why should a clever, hardworking boy who got to a university, got some qualifications for later on in his life, lose out because he's got less time to ride before he becomes 'unconditional' at twenty-five. That's a bad rule.

The conditions of bumper races are bad, too. You need *senior* jockeys riding novice horses. Put a novice on a novice and neither learns anything!

I find the best race jockeys aren't the best schooling jockeys in the world. Other people can ride schooling better. We had two good riders here, Trevor Heath and Adrian Sharp, who never made the grade as jockeys, but they were really excellent when it came to schooling at home. Most jockeys don't like schooling. I gather Fred Winter loathed it. And my Fred who was four times Champion Jockey always used to say, in the years that he rode, that you can know too much about a horse. He would rather go out to the paddock and get on a horse he'd never ridden before in his life, and would probably give it a far better ride. Horses are like lots of things: you can know too much about them!

On Staff

4

Your staff are your friends and you treat them as such. Human nature is such that if you treat people well, hopefully they will reciprocate, the same as if you treat an animal well, it will reciprocate. Maybe we've been lucky, but we had all the staff a tremendous long time. They stuck with us. In fifty years we only ever had four head lads.

You always have a few lads moving about, but it's an advantage of being an isolated yard: you work as a unit and as a family. If you're based in a big training centre, the staff maybe get together in the pub or club, air their grievances, and can walk out of one yard into another. If you're in an isolated place that doesn't happen. Most of the staff at Kinnersley had their own cottages. We supplied them with houses, paid their rent, rates, water rates, everything, which must have been an advantage.

We always tried to keep our staff on full pay for the whole year. We didn't, as they have to do in some jumping yards, ever have to lay any staff off during the summer. They even did the hay-making in the summer, and by the time they'd done the hay-making and had their holidays, the horses were coming in again from grass. That was another advantage of having a farm to run with your yard. You can always find them something to do. You obviously can't afford to pay fifteen or twenty lads to do nothing in the summer.

Some jumping lads like to go into a flat yard for the summer, because they have the chance of doing some winners and earning some more money. But nowadays, when they get three weeks or a month's holiday, and your horses don't go out till the middle or end of May and they're coming in again in the middle of July, the horses are starting roadwork as soon as the lads have had their holiday.

We came by our first head lad, Alf Grazier, because he married the postman's daughter from Kinnersley. He wasn't a local, but he'd been batman to a man called Colonel Christopher in the army, and the Colonel lived locally. Alf came back after the war with him, and wanted a job with horses. It was a natural progression: he worked as a lad in the yard and went on to be head lad. Alf had been in the army in the King's Troop, so although he'd had no racing experience at all, he'd had plenty of experience with horses.

The next head lad was called Barny Hullah, who was a racing lad, who was with us for quite a long time.

The next one we had was Ron Peachey, who was with us in our heyday, during our golden days. He'd also been in the army, and came out of the army to stay with some friends in Kinnersley. His background experience was that his father was a stud groom at the time to Lady Wyfold. So he had plenty of experience with horses and thoroughbred horses. He came as a lad. Then we got him his HGV licence and he progressed to be travelling head lad in the days when Barry Hills was with us.

Barry was serving his apprenticeship at Kinnersley. He had a few rides over hurdles and just one ride over fences. He always laughs about it, for I don't think he really enjoyed it – that was his only ride in a steeplechase. Even in those days Barry was a tremendous character, and madly keen on hunting as a child in the Pony Club with my son Guy. They got into all sorts of horrendous scrapes. They both were banished finally from the Pony Club for a pillow fight in the girls' bedroom. I was told to come and take them both home: 'Forthwith!'

Barry was born in the village of Kinnersley in a house occupied by his father, Bill Hills, who was head lad to Fred's father for a long time, eight or nine years. Then the war came and Kinnersley virtually closed. So Barry went to live with his parents in Upton-on-Severn (his mother was an Upton-on-Severn girl). His father then tried training at Northolt – pony racing at the end of the war. That wasn't a great success. His father didn't have good health and finally he retired. Barry came back to his parents' home and was apprenticed to Fred. But he was always going to be too heavy for a flat race rider, and he wasn't the right sort of person to ride over obstacles. So he went to Newmarket and when Jack Collings subsequently retired, he became travelling head lad to John Oxley.

Barry was always highly intelligent and very sharp. He had a

big gamble on a horse called Frankincense that won the Lincoln in 1968. That really set him up. He had said to Fred prior to the gamble, 'If this comes off I shall be able to set up on my own.' Which in fact he did and he's never looked back. As he has been through the mill, he knows the job backwards, and deserves every bit of the success that he's having.

Once Barry as a lad, and Ron Peachey as travelling head lad, were going racing and they set off with Barry sitting in the back, and Ron driving. One of the horses was being a bit fractious. After they'd only gone a couple of miles, the box stopped and Barry thought, 'Now I've quietened her down, I'll jump in the front.' Whilst he was thinking about jumping in the front, Ron thought he was getting in the back again and drove off and left him! When he got to the races there was no Barry. He was marooned on Dunstall Common.

Ben McCabe, our last head lad, has a racing pedigree. His brother works at the Stackallan Stud in Ireland and Ben came to us when he was only nineteen. He'd worked on the stud a bit in

Fred, in hoop-sleeves on the right, winning at Windsor on Carnival Boy. Frenchie Nicholson is upsides him and in the 1945 season they split the championship.

45

Fred's father (second from the right) at the Champion Jockey's Dinner at The Plough Hotel, Cheltenham, which Fred couldn't go to owing to the fact that he'd broken his neck that afternoon on Coloured School Boy. On Fred's father's right is Lord Mildmay.

Ireland and came to us as an ordinary lad. Then when Ron became ill, Fred picked him out of all the lads we'd got and made him head lad. And though comparisons are odious, he would certainly have been as excellent as any of the others.

Of the various people that work for a trainer – head lad, travelling head lad, jockey, secretary – your head lad is easily the most important. It's rather like being the captain of a ship: it always goes down the line. When the trainer is away – and he is a good deal – the head lad has got to be responsible for everything. You trust him with your horses. Your head lad is vital. He is the one that matters.

A head lad has got to be dedicated to his job because it's a seven day a week job. That's the first thing; he's got to be a worker. The other thing is he's got to be able to manage the staff. You can have some very good lads who do their two or three horses extremely well, but they're not head lad material because you've got to have somebody the staff respect. I think that's the same with an employer. If your staff respect you, you will keep them and the same thing applies to the head lad because he is so responsible he can either hire or fire.

When the trainer's away racing the head lad has got to control the yard. It is essential that you have somebody who is a bit of a loner, who doesn't go down to the local pub every night and consort with all the other lads. He has to be a bit aloof, somebody that they respect, so that when he asks them to do something they do it and don't argue. The same thing applies to an employer. You are friends with all your staff, but you must feel that they respect you. It's a very fine line. You want to be friendly with them, but on the other hand you don't want to invite them up to have a meal with you. Maybe you'd like to, but I don't think you should.

Obviously anybody who works in the yard must have the love of the horse. They have to be dedicated. Somebody like Ben McCabe would love a selling plater just as much as he loved Gaye Brief or Celtic Chief. It's love of an animal really. It's a thing you are born with: animal instinct.

Our famous travelling head lad, Jack Kidd, was a wonderful character. In the days when we lived at Kinnersley, we had a small study-cum-bar. We were having a drink in there one night with some friends when the 'phone rang. A voice said 'This is Jack Kidd speaking' and so Fred in his usual manner said, 'Who the bloody hell is Jack Kidd?' Jack said, 'Jasus Guv'nor, if you saw me, you'd know me. I'm applying for the job as box driver.' Fred asked 'Well, where are you?' Jack said, 'I'm in Jersey.'

Fred liked the direct way Jack had of speaking, so he said 'You'd better come over for an interview.' Jack said 'I'll get a 'plane and I'll be over tomorrow.' So he appeared and was with us for the rest of his life. And he had really got no credentials for being a travelling head lad.

The Kidd family were quite big farmers near Newry, Co. Down in Northern Ireland and they had always had horses, hunters, and point-to-pointers, so he'd always been involved with horses, but not with race horses. He'd been involved with all sorts of other things too, including being a 'Special' in the Ulster Constabulary. I believe he did a fair bit of cattle rustling over the Border; he'd tell horrendous stories of driving cattle over the Border and bullets coming through the van. All sorts of exciting things like that. He was very resourceful and loved animals. One day years ago, we had a horse with colic. 'I know how to cure that, Guv'nor. Get on and ride him down a steep hill, and everything will slip back into place.'

All sorts of weird ideas he had, but he was a marvellous driver and a terrific character. He was unique, Jack was. He'd got hardly any teeth and one day when he was ill and had to go to hospital, Fred was getting his things together and asked, 'Jack, where's your toothbrush?' He said, 'Guv'nor, I haven't got one. I've only got one tooth.' When he was younger he used occasionally to have a bit of a bender, go and have a few drinks, and probably wouldn't show up the next day, but those days were very few and far between. He was a bit of the black sheep of the family at home. Everybody was amazed that he stayed and did what he did. When Fred died, I think he just gave up, and he died the following year. I wonder whether there is still that calibre of old travelling head lads like our Jack Kidd, a remarkable character who knew everybody on the racecourse.

The travelling head lad has got to be resourceful: if the trainer is late getting there, he has got to make up his own mind what he's got to do about running the horses or changing the jockeys. He would have a walk round the course and would be able to say when you arrive 'The ground is not as described: it is either too firm or too heavy.' He would know how your horses had travelled, if one had sweated up or been a nuisance.

But apart from that, Jack Kidd was a larger than life character himself. He used to go and fetch my daughter Scarlett from her boarding school, St James' at Malvern. There was a fierce headmistress in those days called Miss Anstruther. But Jack Kidd got to know Miss Anstruther and used to go and have a glass of sherry with her which the normal run-of-the-mill person would never have been invited to do. But Jack Kidd just knew everyone, and everyone was pleased to see him.

He lived the most extraordinary life in the yard at Kinnersley with all those awful cats. He had eight or nine cats of his own and they lived with him above the stables. The room was horrendous. He used to sort of cook for himself, if you could call it cook, with a filthy frying-pan which the cats used to eat out of. But whenever he went racing, he looked all smart, except occasionally if he was going to a big meeting – he seemed to do it on purpose – and then he might wear his very oldest clothes and an old pair of wellingtons.

Over many, many years, Jack Kidd used to come into the house every night and have a glass of sherry with me and we used to discuss what had happened during the day. If Fred wasn't there, he would always come in. I was very fond of him. And he was very loyal, and when Fred died, I think Jack Kidd just gave up: he

died within nine months. He didn't have anything wrong with him, apart from old age and being worn out. Yet he smoked sixty Park Drive cigarettes a day. Jack was never married. He had a few girl-friends over a period of years, and he had several dramas with them, but those things are best left unsaid. He used to go out as he'd say 'on the town', in Upton, Tewkesbury or Worcester. Local places. And he had many friends. He knew everybody, Jack did.

Once, he found a young trainer's dog loose at Ludlow. She'd escaped from the car. Jack not only knew whose dog it was, but managed to catch her, and then came and told the owners he had got the dog safely. Some people have a natural feeling, a natural instinct for animals. Jack Kidd was one of those, no matter what sort of animal it was. Funnily enough, he rode quite well. He was a very capable rider, which you wouldn't have thought. He rode

Scarlett aged 4 or 5 with Old Mortality who won the Great Yorkshire Chase – then a much more important race than it's now become.

49

out up until the last four or five years, almost until the time Fred died.

When he first became travelling head lad, he was often away with the horses overnight, before the motorways shrunk the country. Jack Kidd is unique in that he drove four National winners to Aintree. He took each one of our National winners (he came to us the year before E.S.B won). Even in the latter years, they used to go up to Liverpool the day before, so he then had the night feeding to do and the looking at the legs. He had a lot of responsibility and rose to all occasions.

He'd ring up from the racecourse stables, as soon as he got up there, to say he had arrived. He'd call Fred, 'Guv'nor'. 'Cheers Guv'nor, it's me.' He always called me 'Madam'. Always. There will never be another Jack Kidd. It would be nice to have a race named after him. In fact, he had his favourite clerks of the courses that he got on well with, and his favourite stewards.

Ben McCabe was excellent as a head lad, but he wasn't the same outgoing character that Jack Kidd was. You would never have Ben in to have a drink with you in the evening. He was a very retiring man and a loner – it's a very good thing if a head lad is like that. Ben was a very dedicated man.

Ron Peachey, our previous head lad, didn't have a frightfully outgoing personality either. He was a quiet man too, those two head lads we had over a period of forty years. In the latter years, I would always be in the yard at five o'clock every afternoon and would go round every horse with Ben. That was 'the thing' at Kinnersley as long as I can remember. Ron would always go round with Fred. But if Fred was away racing, he would always ring Ron up to find out what was right and what was wrong. If there was a drama, he would usually be standing there in the yard waiting for Fred to come. Bad moments . . . But with the quantity of horses that we had over the years – in our heyday, we used to have seventy or eighty winners a year – our dramas were comparatively few. Though everybody who has animals has dramas.

We had several assistant trainers before my last one, John McConnochie, who set up training on his own when I retired in 1989, and I hope he makes a success of it. Our first assistant was Atty Corbert who later became a successful Newmarket trainer, but tragically, was killed in a car accident. If you go back years ago, 'Buster' Harty was assistant and he ended up a leading amateur. He was excellent and then came Will Molony (Tim's son) and then Mathew Delahooke. Then we didn't have one for some years, until Kim Bailey who was here for two seasons when Fred was alive. Kim is now training successfully. He knew a bit before he came to us, for he'd been with Tim Forster, so he wasn't just starting from scratch. Kim was both learning and actually helping us. An assistant should do both.

Then after Kim, after Fred died, I had Michael Bell. I know his parents, and his uncle and aunt live only three miles up the road. He was in the army in those days, and he wanted to ride in the Grand Military. He wanted a horse to ride in it, so we bought him Ten Cherries which subsequently turned out to be a marvellous horse for him. He won the Grand Military on him at Sandown, and then won a few races that season and some more the next season.

Michael wanted to be a trainer and he wanted to have this horse

to ride. He wanted the practical experience of riding races, which is always an excellent idea. He had done six months in France on a stud and then he came to me. He rode for two seasons on his own horse. He 'did' his horse, and another one as well. He was a great worker. When he left me after two seasons, he went to Paul Cole and had two seasons with him, before he started to train on his own. Michael was always very good on the form book and with the entries. He was always switched on. I thought he was a 'natural'.

John McConnochie was here for nine years. He came from South Africa – really for just a month. He knew a friend of Scarlett's in South Africa. He wanted to come to England to a jump trainer, either to Fred Winter or Fred Rimell, and asked this girl if she knew either of them.

She said, 'Well, as a matter of fact, Fred Rimell's daughter is one of my greatest friends.'

So he said, 'Will you ring them up?'

They rang up from Johannesburg and we vaguely said, 'Yes, come.'

We promptly forgot all about it. Then about two months later, we had a phone call from Worcester station, to say 'I have arrived.' The girl, now dead unfortunately, brought him over, and dumped him at Kinnersley and left him. We were faced with a young South African aged twenty-three who had never been out of South Africa.

Kim Bailey left and Johnny automatically stepped into his shoes as an assistant. He was quite a good rider. He hadn't ridden race-riding, but he had ridden a lot of show-jumping in South Africa. He was certainly a very capable horseman, and proved an excellent assistant.

Had I not had a capable assistant after Fred died, I don't think I would ever have taken a licence out, but Johnny had been with us for nearly three years so I obviously knew him well. He knew Fred's ways. In three years you pick up a good deal. He agreed to stay on as assistant to me and it worked very well. The staff have to respect an assistant. They have to feel that the assistant knows what he or she is doing.

Whatever position you're in, you have to have your staff respect you, and then you get on with them and you are friends with them. Possibly that's the reason why we were lucky at Kinnersley to manage to keep our staff for so many years, because they

Scarlett's lap of honour having won the overall Championship at the Royal International Show on Peter Pan at The White City, 1950.

53

respected us. Fred was a very knowledgeable person in all aspects of racing, both riding and training. He had been born into it and gone right through the mill. And I had been virtually right through the mill. I had been married to Fred for forty-four years and I felt that I was fully qualified to take over the licence.

In those days, I rode out every day, so I knew exactly what was happening. Fred didn't ride out after he had broken his neck the last time, so he hadn't ridden for thirty years. But I knew exactly what was happening. Fred always went down in a Range Rover to whatever gallop we were on. I would say to him 'I have entered So-and-So in such-and-such a race on such-and-such a date, do you think he would be ready for then?' And then he would say 'Yes' or 'No'.

I always looked through the entry forms to see what races would suit. I would have a certain horse in mind and I would say 'There, that race would suit him. We must have him ready for then.' And when the weights came out, if we thought we had a fair weight, we would run in it. And if we thought we were badly handicapped, we would say 'We'll declare forfeit and take him out.'

'Mick' Peachey was my secretary for thirty years. She was marvellous. She even worked for me a bit before the war, and was originally married to a jockey called Alec Jack. He made off during the war and abandoned her, and so she took on the secretarial work for me at the very end of the war, and she worked right through for me until 1981. Ron Peachey, who became the head lad, went to stay with friends in the village and eventually married her. So it was quite a good arrangement – we had the secretary and the head lad as a married couple.

After Mrs Peachey died I had another secretary, Toni Gresham, who has now been with me for seven years, so I can't be such a dragon to work for, can I? Otherwise my staff wouldn't have stayed with me as they did.

Fred used to say he simply trained the horses and I did all the entering from that room in the garden which was a bit like a greenhouse. But it proved a very good office. It was really easy, because riding out every day, I knew exactly what the horses were doing, which horses were right, and which horses weren't right, and therefore did all the entries. I used to love looking through the *Racing Calendar* and making up my mind where we were going to run. Fred hated anything like that. He wouldn't even look at the *Calendar*. In fact, I don't think he ever opened it! So it really wasn't a problem: we just seemed to work together.

5   *On Training and Feeding*

We never overworked our horses. But with our National horses, about a week or five days before the race we would give them one really good work-out over a longer distance, possibly over two miles. Normally we would never work a horse over two miles. But if we had a National horse we did, and put another horse in half-way through the gallop. The National horse would jump off with one or two others, and then we'd put another horse in for the last six furlongs to make him really work. Apart from the loose-school, we did very little schooling. Fred always said that every time you schooled a horse, you took a chance. With a horse that has won its races, you get him up from grass for the following season, and when he is fit and ready to have a school, you give him a couple of schools. If he jumps satisfactorily and is a natural jumper that is all you need to do.

Whenever we brought horses over from Ireland and put them in the loose-school, we could tell immediately on that very first outing whether they were dunces or not. Some of them would remain dunces all their lives. Others would be slow to learn, but they would learn.

Our loose-school was an oval. You could put up three fences one side and three fences down the other side. You put poles on the floor to start off a novice first go, and you let him trot round and trot over them. Then you would put them up, not a foot high, and get him used to just hopping over those. Then you gradually increased the height. You nearly always put a pole in front for a take-off line. So you taught him how to take off and how to put himself right. Horses loved it. They would go into the loose-school and would gallop round for fun. They adored it, because they were free. Most horses are natural jumpers, but you do get the odd one that is not a natural jumper, and is ignorant, and so it's hard to teach him and therefore he has to go in a lot.

A long-striding horse is the hardest horse to get to jump, because if he meets a fence on a long stride, he can't put a short one in, so he'll probably stand away a mile, and eventually he's going to get into trouble. But your shorter-striding horse is nearly always a good jumper. We won four Grand Nationals, and three of those horses were short-striding horses. The one that took the long strides was old Rag Trade and he just blundered his way round!

We first saw a loose-school in France, I think at Alec Head's, as far back as when Coloured School Boy ran over there, and when we came back Fred immediately built one, and we used one ever after. It's a wonderful thing because a horse learns to jump naturally. He hasn't got somebody either jabbing him in the mouth, or kicking him up the ribs. He learns to put himself right, he learns to stand off or put in a short one, and he has to do his own thinking. He's not impeded by anybody on his back. If a horse jumps well in the loose-school, by and large he will jump on the racecourse. Normandy, who won eight races on the trot that season, had never been ridden over a hurdle when he ran; he'd only ever been in the loose-school. Then he went to Kempton, jumped off, made all and won. Some horses are natural jumpers – he was – but you get many that aren't. You can do an awful lot for them in the loose-school if you keep at it.

I don't think that a jump trainer should have a licence unless he has a loose-school of his own: that should be brought in as an essential part of being granted a licence.

Coming up from grass in the early days, we used to go on the road for probably an hour and a quarter for six weeks before they ever went on the grass. But in latter years, we kept off the roads, principally because the roads have got an increasing volume of traffic. Surfaces have become slippy. At Kinnersley we were fortunate enough to have a large quantity of land and plenty of places to ride, so that you could do your work on the grass, up hills without ever having to go on the roads. Hammering and trotting along the road produces a few problems like splints. If you can get on the roads you'd better just walk for three weeks. After that, you would be better trotting about in the fields.

I always rode out myself. We would trot for, say, a quarter of an hour, and then we would walk for a quarter of an hour and then

Left to right: *Three champion National Hunt Jockeys – Fred, Bryan Marshall, Mary Marshall (she was Mary Whitehead then) and Tim Molony at the Royal International at The White City.*

we would trot again. When we started them cantering, we would hack very slowly for another three weeks. It takes three months to get a horse ready to run. On occasions we've done it in less time; horses all vary. Some will come twice as quick as others. Some are very active: they work and get themselves fit.

The majority of our horses were turned out at Kinnersley in the summer. Some would go back to their owners if they had land and could have them at home. But Fred always liked to keep them at Kinnersley if he could, because they were always looked at twice a day. As soon as you turn a horse out, you get just as many problems with feet and all sorts of things as you do when it is in. You need to keep them under your eye.

We would turn them out when the grass was nice in May and June, and possibly in July, and then we would feed them for the last two or three weeks out in the field. The idea is that whatever condition they've got, they hold it. Because I never think horses do well after the middle of July. If you are going to leave them out until August, they want feeding with a bit of hard corn or nuts inside them.

I fed in exactly the same way that Fred fed. Because the head lad that I inherited from Fred, Ben McCabe, was head lad at Kinnersley for nineteen years. Obviously we went on in the same way. He would feed every horse in the yard at half past six in the morning. They would all have their breakfast and the First Lot would go out at eight o'clock and they would be fed again when they came in from exercise by half past nine. Then the Second Lot would go out and they would be fed when they came in from exercise. And if you had a Third Lot, they would be fed when they came in. And then they would be tied up at four o'clock, dressed over and then fed again at six. They were always fed three times a day with the big feed at night.

Horses vary with their appetites. By and large, we would give them as much as they could eat. Fred was always a great believer in very good hay, and giving them as much as they would eat, because it is the bulk feed. In latter years, I bought all the hay. I was lucky to be able to buy most of the hay locally. Different farmers that I knew, always knew they had got a customer if they had got good hay. So it was virtually made with Kinnersley in mind. I very seldom had to go outside to a dealer. It was always bought direct from the farms.

You want a good mixture of rye-grass and clover. And you don't want soft hay, what I call 'cattle' hay. It wants to be nice and bright, so that when you break it, it crackles. It wants to gleam. And you must hold hay until Christmas. That applies to oats too: old hay and old oats. After Christmas, you can go onto the last crop. That has become a necessity, because it has been increasingly difficult to buy good old hay and good old oats. You should try to buy hay that the farmer hasn't sprayed. Sprays could possibly be responsible for one or two viruses, so therefore you try to buy from people that you know haven't been spraying with all sorts of horrible things.

We bought the oats from Scotland, always. We never could get any good oats locally. A good oat wants to have plenty of weight about it and not be all husk: it wants to have a good middle. And they want to be clean. We always used to buy them already cleaned and used to crush oats every day so that we were always using newly crushed oats. We always only *cracked* them. We used to buy them whole in sacks – I'd buy twenty tons at a time – and they would all go up into the loft. Then every morning they would be crushed to the quantity that we wanted to use that day. Freshly cracked, so our bin would be virtually empty at half past six at night, with just enough for the half past six feed the next morning. Then they would be crushed ready for our First Lot to be fed when they came in from exercise.

We used to give our horses a mash, boiled linseed and oats, twice a week – Tuesdays and Saturdays, boiling the oats and linseed together. We had two of those big lined boilers, German, I think, so that the mash couldn't burn. It would be put on in the morning and then they would be ready to make the mash at night. In latter years we used quite a few mineral and vitamin additives, and a bit of honey which I think is good for them. The horses loved it. Some horses would have a mixture of oats and nuts, some horses would have all oats and some horses would have all nuts. It depended on what they would eat.

They all had a salt lick and we used to give them made-up salts twice a week. We used to make our own potion up and they would have a jam jar of it in their water. It was a very good mixture of Epsom, glauber and common salts. You just put it in a big bucket and melt it down with boiling water and then take a jam jar out and put it in their water. It was only weak, so they really didn't taste it. In fact, I think they quite liked it: It would slightly flush their kidneys, keep them healthy and keep all the humour away, so that hopefully you wouldn't get big legs on a Monday morning, and exciting things like that!

We probably had less leg trouble than many trainers. Certainly, the vet (who'd only been coming here five or six years) seemed to think we had had fewer colic problems and that sort of thing than a lot of people. Whether that's been luck, I can't tell. We haven't had a great quantity of problems, but as I say, as long as you have horses, you'll have problems.

As to legs: I hate bandages, but I love the hose pipe. If we thought they required it when they came back from work, we would run the hose on their legs. The great thing with legs is to stop them completely with the first hint of a problem. It is no use trying to hide it, saying, 'We'll give it three or four days, and then it'll be all right.' You've got to stop completely.

Today, of course, you've got the scan, so you know immediately what sort of a problem you've got. Whereas in the old days, we didn't have it. It is only in the last couple of years that the scan has come into being to tell you instantly how much of a problem you have got, and what the damage is. The vet has a scanner, but I'd imagine if you had a big yard with a lot of horses, you'd probably have your own. The vet would come to me and scan a horse, and it was easy to understand after he had explained it. It was quite easy to read. The scan will tell you immediately whether you've got a strain or a blow, or how much bruising there is.

I hate bandages because I think they create more trouble than they ever cure. You only ever have one person in a hundred who is capable of putting a bandage on correctly. I just don't like them. They could be put on too tight, and a lot of trouble has been done over the years. We very seldom used bandages.

But we hardly ever ran a horse of ours without boots. Boots wouldn't ever help a horse if it has got a leg problem, but they certainly prevent an injury. If they are going to strike into themselves – which a horse often would do with a hind leg – it lessens the injury. So therefore it's a preventative. We had all sorts of boots. The best boots in the end were the old leather boots which were lined with rubber, but today there are so many variations of boots, it's a case of trial and error. Those little light felt boots that we used to run Gaye Brief in were lovely. They were light but Gaye Brief never had a leg problem of any description.

Boots in heavy ground might get damp and heavy – and they would weigh a bit. But there were certain boots which I felt didn't. And in heavy ground you can so easily get a horse striking into himself, that you have got to decide whether it's worthwhile leaving the boots off or keeping them on.

The particular sort of bridle that Fred used to love was the three piece bridle. We always knew them as 'three-piece'. They have got a piece in the middle with two joints so you've got a flat bit. It was a very comfortable bit for a horse, and a fairly good thick bit, too. Fred hated thin bits, because he always thought they were uncomfortable for the horse. We used a tremendous lot of rubber bits, and ran a lot of horses in them. They were a much kinder bit.

We very seldom put on a lot of gadgets. Quite often, we'd use the Australian rubber noseband which would just keep the bit high in the horse's mouth if it were apt to get its tongue over it. We seldom used a tongue strap. I hated them; they are horrid things. Very occasionally, we'd use a drop noseband on a horse

that pulled or got its mouth open. We nearly always ran our horses in nosebands. If we had a horse that was a bit what I call 'gobby', sticking its nose up, we would let the noseband down and put it on fairly tight.

We always used breast plates or breast girths. A breast girth was good for the sort of narrow-gutted horse whose saddle was apt to go back badly, otherwise we used a breast plate. I don't think we ever ran a horse without them. They were standard equipment for us, and our breast plate always had a type of elastic in it, half-way down so that it had got plenty of leeway. And the breast girth had elastic on it at the end.

As to shoeing, the only thing we used to do – when the ground was very firm – was to put cork underneath the shoes. You can get that gasket-cork they used on motor cars and put that under. It would be like wearing a sock in your shoes. It didn't cover the sole of the foot, just simply where the shoe was. It was cut out so it was completely under the shoe. Fred always thought it used to take a bit of the jar out.

It's not so much that you need a lot of land to train jumpers: you want variation. Horses are a bit like humans: you've got to have a routine, but you want variations in your routine. The horses want feeding at the same time, want to go out and exercise at the same time, they want tying up in the afternoon at four o'clock and dressing over, and feeding at six o'clock. That is a routine that you must stick to. Then your horses know what they're doing: they know they're going to rest in the afternoon, so they'll eat, and they will be relaxed.

But as far as their exercise is concerned, you should try to vary your exercise in different places. That keeps them interested and they enjoy it. I don't mean that you set off and jump them off in different places, and get them out so that they don't know if they're going to jump off here or jump off there. That makes them permanently excited. That's the last thing you want to do. At Kinnersley, speaking for myself and Fred, I can't remember the last time we had a sweaty, excitable horse that was a nuisance. They shouldn't be 'geed up', if they're relaxed and they're mentally right. There are some excitable horses and you have exceptions to every rule, the same as you have some excitable human beings. But the bulk of your horses should be quiet and relaxed, they shouldn't sweat and steam. They should be able to go out and work, and almost anybody should be able to ride them.

Fred's uncle W.J. (Will) Rimell who was a great help to Fred in the early days. He owned horses and gave Fred a lot of encouragement.

Of course, I'll miss the training. I'll miss the getting up in the morning and going out every morning of my life at eight o'clock. I'll miss seeing the horses work, seeing them in the evening at five o'clock, seeing whether I think they're 'doing' or 'not doing', seeing whether the legs are right or not right.

I shan't miss going round feeling the legs when one's got a bit of heat in it – I shan't miss that! I shall miss the routine. I shall miss the chat. The chat's great – of course it is. The gossip and the chat, I shall miss all that enormously.

The worst thing about training is the owners. I've always thought that. They come back for the weekend at five o'clock on a Friday, and they think, 'Ah, I've got a horse in training! I'll ring up the trainer, we'll go and see it.' Whereas the trainer is working seven days a week, and there's no day you can say, 'Well, I'll have a day off.' But you get the recompenses for it and the pleasure from it. You enjoy your work. Whatever you do in life, there's going to be something you don't like, no matter what you do. You've always got to have hardships and crosses to bear, and if you're doing a job you enjoy doing, well, don't moan.

The nicest thing is going and buying a nice young horse, bringing it back and being really pleased with it when you get it back. Not when you get it home, thinking 'God, why did I buy it!' But when it works out, and when the first time it goes and wins – that gives you the most enormous amount of satisfaction. The trainer probably gets more pleasure from it than the owner even, because he's seen the horse all the way through, and been responsible for buying it. It's your baby, as a trainer. It's like your child.

If you're starting out as a trainer, the first thing you want to do is get some good owners. And then you want to buy them some good horses. You get the good owners in a personal way. You've got to know people quite well who are interested in racing and who you feel would like to have a horse. If you get the complete novice owner, then you have probably got to buy him a different type of horse – the sort of horse that Martin Pipe is running, the ex-flat horse that you know will go and win something, some-where. Maybe it's only going to be at Taunton or Hereford, but the thing is they want to have a winner. Then if you can get something to win, you can probably buy them a nicer sort of a horse, that will eventually graduate to becoming a 'chaser. You can't *buy* a 'chaser, unless you are prepared to give fortunes. I don't think you could ever buy a ready-made 'chaser. They are always a very scarce thing, unless you have an unlimited amount of money. So therefore you have to make your 'chasers. If you're lucky enough to have the right owner, you ought to buy something that you *hope* will go on and become a 'chaser, not just a hurdle-race horse.

If I was setting up in this day and age with all these claiming races on the flat I would have a go at some of them. There are plenty of nice three-year-olds that you could go and claim for ten or fifteen thousand. Whether you'd be too unpopular, I don't know! But everybody's got their own life to live, and if people put horses into claiming races, they must be prepared to have them claimed.

I would go and have a bash at about a dozen of those, if I could. And then go and buy a few nice young horses to fall back on. Your old handicappers are always the backbone of your yard. You can have all your novices, but in the end your old handicappers are the backbone. Even if they're not world-beaters, they win races. They'll win two or three races each season. Whereas you get all excited about a nice novice, probably quite expensive, and you'll probably win just one race with him.

If you've got a young person or a new person coming into racing, don't buy them one of these backward horses so that you're going to have to say 'Well, I may be able to give him just two races this season, and then the next season, we *may* have a nice horse.' Because they're going to get fed up. They are going to get fed up with waiting and fed up with paying the bills. But they can go and get a quick return by getting something out of a claiming race.

On Owners 6

Fred was marvellous at talking to the owners, which is the thing that I was never much good at. He had endless patience and should have been a diplomat. When we came back after a disappointing day when the owner hadn't been able to get there and you had thought the horse was going to run well and it had run abysmally, Fred would ring up the owner, talk to him, tell him what he thought and think of all sorts of reasons why it hadn't run well. And to the best of his ability they would be truthful reasons. He was also capable of making the whole thing *fun* for owners, which is the primary thing. You have to do that: they're in N.H. racing for pleasure as opposed to flat racing, which *is* a business.

That's the difference: one is a sport, and the other's a business. Today flat racing has become even more of a business, because there is so much money involved. I don't personally think the Arab influence in flat racing is a bad thing; they've done many good things for it. They've created a lot of employment. They've kept the best blood in the U.K. But on the other hand, smaller owners who – let's be honest – are the back-bone of racing, get slightly fed up with seeing 'maroon body and white sleeves' or 'blue with white epaulettes' all the time winning their races.

We had the first Arab in National Hunt racing. Sheikh Ali, as we called him – Sheikh Ali Abu Khamsin. We met him at Chepstow. It was quite funny. We were sitting having a drink with our owners – we'd just had a couple of winners – and he sent over a man he employed in those days who had a beard who said 'Sheikh Ali would like you to go and speak to him.'

I asked Fred, 'Who do you think he is?'

Fred said 'Probably the camel driver!'

However, it proved to be a very happy relationship, and he was a very good owner, a frightfully easy man to train for because he left you completely alone. The only stipulation he ever made was

Tim Molony riding Unconditional Surrender who was the first horse we ever bought as trainers. He subsequently won 29 races. We gave 210 guineas for him. Black horses were always lucky for us because Gaye Chance, Corunna and Overland were all black.

hopefully to have runners at the National Hunt Meeting at Cheltenham because that was the one time of the year that he was always in the U.K. And I was fortunate because I won him a Champion Hurdle. I won him an Arkle. In 1989, my last Cheltenham, I was second for him in the Ritz with Gala's Image.

Apart from the fact that he had good horses, he was a lucky owner. Nearly everything he had won. He was lucky for me, for Fred Winter and for Les Kennard who started him off. It was because he used to leave it to you. You could run them where you liked. And he had a retained jockey, Richard Linley, with whom I was fortunate enough to get on very well. I liked him as a person and I liked him as a rider: it was an excellent arrangement.

All the years I've been racing, my experience is that if your owners leave you alone and provided you have luck, you win races for them. But as soon as they start to interfere, it's disaster. When they want to run it in a different race or at a different meeting, or they want a different rider. If they don't win they have to blame somebody. They usually pick on the rider first and the trainer next. And as soon as you get those sort of owners, they never meet with a lot of success. But on the other hand, you do have lucky owners – of that I'm convinced.

I don't think the lucky owner is necessarily lucky in other things, it's not just a lucky man or a lucky woman. You can have somebody who has done terribly well business-wise, and can be frightfully unlucky owning racehorses. And the bad luck runs on year after year. I didn't find it happened more often with poorer people who we hoped would win.

There were plenty of people who were financially very well off like Sir George Dowty, who was a charming man. He left it completely to us and he spent a lot of money on horses. But, though he was a brilliant businessman, he wasn't a lucky owner. The two don't run together.

Charlie Hambro, who also left it completely to us, didn't have as many horses as George Dowty did, but he had quite a few horses. They were all bought with good intentions, and very good horses we thought, but disaster seemed to strike in all sorts of different directions.

The first horse Charlie ever had was a half-share in a horse with a farmer friend. The horse was called Floater and it ran in Charlie's name in a novices' chase at Birmingham. Fred said to Charlie, 'I think this horse will win.' It was coming to the last, and it was twenty lengths in front. Charlie was standing near to Fred and said, 'I can't look, I can't look! I'm closing my eyes.'

So Fred said, 'For God's sake open your eyes! You may never have another winner!'

In fact it did win, it jumped the last and won very easily. Charlie was a delightful character, but just not a lucky owner.

My worst day's racing ever was obviously when Fred broke his neck for the second time at Cheltenham. That was horrific. But my worst day's racing when I was training was when I went to Cheltenham with Very Promising. I'd bought him in Ireland for £18,000 and had won six races on the trot with him the previous season, finishing up by winning the big novices at Liverpool, and then the 'Players' at Chepstow – it was a big race then for five-year-olds only, the W.D. & H.O. Wills series. The following year he obviously wasn't an easy horse to place because he'd won a high value in stake money per race, and also he was top of the handicap.

He belonged to a very tiresome owner called Bob Mann, who was an ex-football referee. He had been terribly lucky. He'd had another horse called Masterson who'd never stopped winning for him, also trained by me. In fact he'd won a big novices final at Cheltenham, a £10,000 race. I went to Cheltenham and Very Promising ran in the Champion Hurdle. It was a horrid day for me anyway because Gaye Brief had gone wrong: he had done something to his back and couldn't run. I ran Very Promising and he ran a marvellous race in the Champion Hurdle to be third.

About an hour later, Anthony Stroud who is now Sheikh Mohammed's manager, came to me and said 'Do you know Very Promising has been sold?'

I couldn't believe it. I was knocked for six. Had I known the horse was for sale, I think I could have found an owner in the yard who would have bought him. Anyway, I couldn't believe anyone would do such a thing without telling me. I said, 'I can't believe it.'

He said, 'Oh yes, he has. He's been bought, and David Nicholson has bought him for John Maunders.'

That really was a body blow, because he was a very good horse. I'd bought him, he'd won a lot of races, and he'd certainly repaid his value several times over, and I couldn't believe anyone could behave in such a manner. It was all new to me. The whole thing was rushed through, and the horse was vetted the next day and

Tim Molony winning the National Hunt Handicap at Cheltenham (now called The Ritz Chase) on Landfort which belonged to Harvey Oliver whose brother originally owned E.S.B. and whose son is Henry Oliver. Lying second is Dick Francis on Lord Bicester's famous Silver Fame.

went. And that for me was the end of Very Promising. So I was obviously very upset, because he was one of the best horses I had in the yard, and good ones are few and far between, and I hadn't got that many horses anyway.

For me there were no other deals done by owners like that. No one removed their horses in a temper. Over the years, a few people have taken horses away, but only very seldom. That's really the most unpleasant thing that has happened to me in the last ten years. I really can't comment on whether I liked the man up till then. He'd been remarkably lucky.

Ted Wheatley, the owner of Comedy of Errors on the other hand was a splendid man – one of those who left you completely alone. You were allowed to do exactly as you wished. He walked into the office one day, and said to Fred, 'I want you to buy me a horse.' We'd never seen him before, but he came with a very old owner of ours, whom he knew only very slightly.

Fred asked, 'What sort of money?'

He said, 'Oh, I don't know, £30,000, £40,000!' Which was huge money in those days.

We were sending a horse, Innismaan, over to run in the Irish Sweeps – he was subsequently second in it. I was talking to Dick Waugh who used to work for the CBA and is now a stud manager, and said, 'Dick, you don't happen to know where there's a decent young horse for sale?'

70

He said, 'Yes, I do. A horse called Comedy of Errors,'

I speedily looked it up and I saw it was trained by Tom Corrie, so I rang Dick back and I said 'I don't think Tom will sell him.'

'Oh yes,' he said, 'he's for sale.'

Corrie was then training himself near Shrewsbury, but the horse was owned by a man who was a veterinary surgeon. I again said that I didn't think he'd sell him.

'Oh yes, he's definitely for sale, we have him on our books.'

So then Fred rang Tom Corrie, who immediately said he wasn't for sale. So Fred rang Dick Waugh back, and said 'Tom Corrie says he's not.'

Waugh said 'Oh, yes he is.'

Fred said, 'I'd like to go and see him tomorrow.'

Dick said, 'I'll make the arrangements.'

When we went and saw him on the Sunday, Tom was really very nice. Obviously he didn't want to lose the horse. The owner, Mr Jarvis the vet, came and we bought the horse there and then. I think we gave £10,000 for him. And the rest is history!

Ted Wheatley subsequently turned out to be the most super owner. The only thing that was slightly bothering, when we had bought him was when he said, 'I'm going to give him to my best friend, Harold Plotnik.' Whereupon Fred almost had a coronary, because he knew that Harold Plotnik had had horses with various other trainers. So he thought he might lose him. He didn't want him to have Comedy. He had wanted Ted Wheatley to have him. So he talked to Ted, and Ted said 'All right, I'll just give him half.'

So he gave the half of him to Harold Plotnik who subsequently turned out to be an equally good owner and he ran in joint names. The horse was the best horse, for all the races he won, we ever had at Kinnersley.

Ted Wheatley was the most generous owner. Not only did he give Fred a gold cup, the replica of the Champion Hurdle, he also gave a gold cup to the jockey Ken White, the year he won it. The second time the horse won the Champion Hurdle Ted took Fred and me on a cruise on the *QE2*. He was a wonderful owner, and he's still a friend. He was in the property business, and in carpets. Plotnik had always been interested in racing, and Ted Wheatley, who knew nothing about racing, had suddenly decided he wanted to have a horse – Comedy happened to be the horse. He is the owner who stands out.

Bryan Jenks, now living in Monte Carlo, was a tremendous

owner. We had a lot of fun with Bryan, in those halcyon days when Bryan was leading owner and we had super horses for him. He was a wonderful owner because again he left you completely alone. His wife had a horse with me my last season.

He was introduced to us by the man who owned Nicolaus Silver, Jeremy Vaughan. We knew Jeremy because his father Douglas owned Last of the Dandies who was second in the National, trained by Fred's brother-in-law, Gerry Wilson. Jeremy's one ambition was to go one better than father and win the National. Father of course never forgave him!

When we bought Nicolaus Silver, Jeremy was with us in Dublin. Fred was already in Ireland, and Jeremy and I had been to Wolverhampton, where Jeremy had got absolutely plastered. We flew from Liverpool, and he snored all the way up in the car, an absolute menace. I couldn't wait to get him on the 'plane. As a matter of fact, I didn't think they'd let him on the 'plane, but anyway they did. And when we eventually arrived at Dublin I just hoped Fred would be there to meet us. Jeremy staggered down the steps, and I was able to pass him over to Fred.

When I saw Ivor Herbert there at Ballsbridge Sales with his owner, the film producer Frank Launder, I knew he was our opposition. I just wondered whether he knew the horse was qualified for the Grand National*, because in those days you had to have a qualification. *I* knew he was qualified but I wondered if anybody else knew. We bought Nicolaus Silver with the National specifically in mind because Jeremy was absolutely demented to go one better than his father. The only race that Jeremy wanted to win was the Grand National, because his father had been second in it. They didn't get on frightfully well and it was one-up-manship. And it worked out that way.

The first winner we ever trained was for Count Paul Munster. We were up at a gymkhana near Bridgenorth. In those days when we were starting fifty years ago, Fred used to have a very good gymkhana pony. The pony was a small source of livelihood for us: we had to make use of everything. The Munsters met Fred there,

---

* Indeed I did, for the horse had been strongly recommended to me by his late trainer's stable-jockey, Jimmy Morrissey, to whom I'd given a job. Dan Kirwan, who had trained Nicolaus Silver, had suddenly died which was why the horse was on the market. It turned out that both Fred Rimell and I had the same limit: 2,500 gns. I had the 2,400 bid, so Fred could cap it. I.H.

but he didn't know them and didn't remember their names.

One evening we were sitting in the little bar at Kinnersley and the telephone rang and a voice said, 'This is Count Paul Munster speaking.'

So Fred said, 'And I'm the bloody King of England.' I can always remember it.

He said, 'No, I *am* Paul Munster and I've got a horse called Good Date I want you to take.'

Paul Munster was German and he was married to Lady Stavordale's sister. Subsequently we became very friendly with both of them and the rest of the family. Charlie Hornby, who was a nephew of theirs, was assistant trainer to us for three or four years. The horse came and the first race we ever won as trainers was with Good Date at Taunton. You think about these things many years later, don't you?

Frank Jordison, another early owner, was a splendid man. He had Unconditional Surrender, and lots of other good horses, like Red Mead. In fact he was our first owner – though not our first winner – and Unconditional Surrender was the very first horse that we bought. We bought him at Newmarket for the princely sum of 210 gns and he had sore shins all season. Every time we were going to run him in a hurdle race we couldn't. So in the end the first race we ever won with him was a novice chase at Worcester. He won it, and went on and won twenty-nine races: he was a very talented big black two-mile horse.

Frank Jordison, the most amusing owner we ever had by a mile, was our first owner with Unconditional Surrender, Corunna, Red Mead, Overland. Nearly all his whole string won. And he was a comedian really, just a funny little man. To look at him you'd have thought him a nonentity. But he owned a string of hotels. He had no family, no children, and he was just keen on racing. He knew a lot about it, was a very good judge, and very good on the form book. He would always tell you what you had got to beat in a race, and he was nearly always right.

One day Frank Jordison was talking to Colonel Dick Holland, who was the senior stipendiary steward. Colonel Holland remarked, 'Mr Jordison, I see you've retired your old horse, Unconditional Surrender.'

Frank said, 'Yes. You know, he won me twenty-nine races – and on two occasions he wasn't trying but he won both!'

In those days that was quite amusing because stipendiary

E.S.B. ridden by Tim Brookshaw winning The Grand Sefton Trial Steeplechase at now defunct Hurst Park, after he had won the National.

stewards weren't quite the calibre they are today. But luckily Colonel Holland was a particularly nice 'stipe'.

We went to Ireland the following year to buy another horse for Frank Jordison. We flew to Dublin in this horrid little 'plane Jordison had chartered just for us, to Collinstown. In those days there were no runways. We landed on the grass and the 'plane nose-dived and got stuck. Jordison was a nervous man who hated flying anyway, so he consumed a lot of brandy on the way over. We drove round Ireland and saw about twenty or thirty horses and in the end he said, 'I don't care what the next horse looks like, buy it. I'm not looking at any more.'

And the next horse was another black horse called Overland. He also turned out to be a very good horse and won lots of races. The next horse we bought for him was yet another black horse called Corunna. Frank and I went to Wolverhampton where the horse was running in a seller. It wasn't the done thing to claim a horse out of a seller. It was odds on ridden by Michael Beary, but it got left and got beaten into second place, and Frank claimed it. When we got back, Fred was absolutely furious that we'd claimed this horse. 'I wouldn't have done it!' he said angrily to me. He wouldn't have allowed Frank to have done it, but I had let him.

We ran him the first time in a mile and a half three-year-old hurdle at Cheltenham (in those days three-year-old hurdles were only a mile and a half). He won, and subsequently won no end of races. It was a funny thing that Frank had three good horses with us, all jet black.

The other good horse we had in those early days was Comique, who belonged to a chap called Reg Coombes, who ran a taxi service and was the Mayor of Torquay. Comique won us about thirty races and we bought him as a four-year-old at Newmarket for about 340 guineas. He was an ex-J.V. Rank horse, trained by old Noel Cannon on the flat. He'd been a very good two-year-old, but useless as a three-year-old, and he was a crib-biter and a wind-sucker! They used to put all these terrible gadgets on him to prevent him. Fred bought him and left everything off him. He wouldn't use any of these horrible neck straps or any prevent-atives. The only thing we ever did, was to tie him up short on the morning of his race. He was placed in the Gold Cup.

We took Comique to Newton Abbott because that was Reg Coombes' home meeting. In those days the spring tide used to flood the course and one day on the morning of racing the course

was flooded. Fred went up to ride the horse work and he was cantering him around through the water. Several trainers and other people who were standing down there watching, said 'What's that lunatic doing? Cantering that horse through water!'

Came the race, and there was only one horse that galloped through the water – that was Comique because he'd already had the experience that morning. So he won and Fred had the last laugh.

Sir George Dowty, a very nice person, often used to stay with us when we still lived in Severn Stoke. We had a marvellous girl, Nora, working in the house, who worked for me for fourteen years. One morning she came in laughing her head off. I said, 'What's so funny then?'

She said, 'I've just taken in Mr Dowty '(as he then was)' a cup of tea, and there was an eye looking at me out of the glass.'

He had a glass eye which he apparently used to take out at night. Nora, an Irish girl, was laughing her head off. 'Jasus! There was this eye staring at me!'

He was a wonderful, but unlucky, owner. He had a decent horse called Tokoroa who didn't belong to him originally. He first belonged to a person I wasn't very keen on called Dave Deyong, a bookmaker. He was bought for Deyong. The first time he backed him, he got beaten. Deyong said he'd sell him. Fred said to George, 'I think this is a really decent horse; would you like to buy him?'

George said, 'Yes, I'll have him.'

He did win George a lot of races and he was second in the 1958 Champion Hurdle to Bandalore. Dave Dick rode him that day and I always thought he should have won it. Dave Dick, in annoyance, picked his whip up after the horse had gone past the post two lengths behind the winner and hit him across the ears which infuriated me. I don't think Dave, who had ridden E.S.B when he won the National in 1956, ever rode for us again.

Tokoroa won over fences at Newbury when George Dowty had remarried a Canadian girl, the present Lady Dowty. She wasn't very interested in racing anyway, and Fred rang them up and said, 'George, I want to run the horse at Newbury, I think he'll win. He's in a novices' chase.'

George said, 'Well, I can't go.'

Fred said, 'I'm *sure* you can go. What's the problem?'

'No,' he said, 'I can't go.'

Guy on a show pony called Melody who was subsequently sold to America where he won at Madison Square Gardens.

He had a very good secretary called Judy, who rang afterwards and said, 'Fred, do you know why he won't go? He's been invited to go shooting tomorrow and so he's got a man coming up here with some clays. He's going to practise.'

It turned out to be a very foggy day, so in the end he had the clays put up outside the window of his drawing-room and he shot out of the window at them. Judy went to Newbury and Tokoroa won his first chase. He was a very good horse, subsequently killed over fences.

We had several seconds in the Champion Hurdle. Spartan General was second in 1965 to Kirriemuir and we always thought he should have won it. Terry Biddlecombe rode him and he thought afterwards he should have won. Bryan Jenks said to Fred one day, 'You'll never win the Champion Hurdle, it's an unlucky race for you.' Then, of course, we won it three times.

Mr Highman was a funny man who bought Coloured School Boy for the price of a sack of oats, about a fiver. Fred was riding Comique at Fontwell and won the race. During the race he saw this horse in these black and yellow wasp-striped colours, come cruising upsides him, and thought how well it was going. The next thing, it fell. That very night, this man Highman rang up and said, 'I've got two horses. Would you have them?'

Fred asked 'What are they?'

He told him. Fred said, 'Yes, I'll have him, because I saw him during the race and know how well he was going.'

The other one was useless so we sent him back.

Coloured School Boy was a bag of bones when he arrived. We summered him well. He was a horse with a terrific amount of ability and won a lot of races. Unfortunately he didn't have very good legs. Had he been a sound horse he would have won a lot more. It was that horse, Coloured School Boy, that broke Fred's neck for the last time in the Gold Cup.

At one time Bryan Jenks would have had probably eight or ten horses with us, and was leading owner in the 1968–69 season with nine horses winning twenty-five races. We had some very good horses in those days. At the National Hunt Meeting, races are very hard to win, but in 1969 we won the Triumph Hurdle with Coral Diver, we won one division of what was called the Gloucester Hurdle in those days (now the Waterford Crystal) with Normandy. And we were second in the 1969 Gold Cup with Domacorn and they all belonged to Bryan Jenks. We also won the

Arkle with Chatham, a horse of somebody else's, so we had a wonderful National Hunt Meeting.

Bryan was a great owner: he left it entirely to us and was prepared to give a good price for a horse. We got on tremendously well and he certainly was one of the nicest owners we ever had.

Harry Collins, a splendid man, was a great character. He sent his horse, Woodland Venture, to us and he really was a horrible horse. He was nappy, and didn't want to go anywhere, and didn't want to do anything. And he was a bad jumper. We had a very good lad working for us in those days called Graham Nicholls, and I honestly think Fred would have given up with the horse if it hadn't been for Graham, and possibly for me. He was the sort of horse who had to have something in front of him all the time because he didn't want to go anywhere or do anything. Somehow or other one always sensed that the horse had ability and Graham really made the horse.

One day we were down at Harry Collins' place in Dorset where he was a big dairy farmer. We went into his sitting room and saw an alcove made of stone in the corner. It was empty. I said to him laughingly, 'Harry, what are you going to put in there?'

He said, 'The Gold Cup!'

I asked, 'Who's going to win it?'

He said, 'Woodland Venture.'

And Woodland Venture when he came to us had run in just three point-to-points and had fallen in two and had pulled up in the other; and Harry decided that he was going to win the Gold Cup! Which he did! Graham Nicholls and Terry made the horse. Nobody else would have put up with him, other than Terry, who was wonderful on a young horse in those days.

Sir Edward Hanmer had had horses at Kinnersley since 1936 when Fred's father trained for him, so he spanned two lifetimes. Sir Edward was a very severe man, very strait-laced, but a very fair man – always slightly frightening. In my youth I was terrified of him. As the years went on I got to know him a lot better and became very friendly with him. He left me all his stud books, the whole set of them from when they were first printed, but unfortunately they were in our office at Kinnersley when it burnt down and nearly all of them were destroyed.

David Brown, who was the owner of Linwell that Ivor Herbert trained, was amongst the tycoons I'd have known. We did train a horse for him but it was never very successful. He wasn't a real racing man. He only had a horse, I think, because it was the thing to do. He was a little bit tight with his money, and he wasn't a particularly likeable character.

Our connection with the strange 'Teazy-Weazy' Raymond, was that in the days when Fred was riding he used to ride for him. He'd known him for many years. Teazy-Weazy bought Rag Trade at Doncaster Sales and ran him in that year's Grand National when he was trained by somebody else and John Francome rode him.

Teazy-Weazy then rang Fred up and asked him if he would take a horse during the summer whose objective was the National. Fred said he would. John Burke, who was the most beautiful horseman, rode the horse to win the Welsh Grand National and then the Liverpool National. I don't think many riders would have won the National on him because he was really not a particularly nice horse: he would simply gallop right through a fence. He was a great big common horse who looked like a Suffolk Punch. But he stayed and, if you had the right rider on him, which we were lucky enough to have in John Burke, you had a chance. Of all the jockeys that we had riding over so many years, John Burke with beautiful hands was the best horseman. He wouldn't have had the flair of Terry, or been the opportunist that Terry was.

Teazy-Weazy as a person was a very difficult man, and it was very acrimonious dissolving the partnership with him. We won the National and that was about the end of it: the horse was sold after that. Rag Trade was the only horse we ever had of his, and he had sent him to us, I suppose, because we had won three Nationals and he thought we had a good National record.

Another tycoon we had was Maxwell Joseph. But, like David Brown, he only really had a horse because it was the thing to do, and he wasn't very successful. But subsequently his first wife, Sybil, had quite a bit of success. We won her a Welsh National with a horse called Glenn, and she had two or three quite good horses. But though she was always quite keen, by then he took no interest in it at all.

Tycoon owner types can be irritating. If you have a very successful man, like Maxwell Joseph who was an enormously successful businessman, they think that if they pay a lot of money they are going to be successful whatever they do. There's a tremendous amount of luck in buying horses. No matter what you give for a horse, it isn't necessarily going to buy success. George

Dowty was a good owner, but wasn't a lucky owner, though we had lots of winners for him. He was prepared to spend the money. Maxwell Joseph wasn't prepared to spend the money and he wasn't lucky either. I don't think he really had any interest in racing.

With all horses you can set off and find that with the best will in the world you have problems. Horses have so many problems that you've got to be lucky. Greta Lyons was quite lucky. She had a good horse called Jungle Beach and he won her about a dozen races. She had another horse called Playschool, who also won for her. But I think the Lyons thought that horses were like the motor cars, (Sir William Lyons was head of Jaguar and our son Guy was married to his daughter). They though that whatever they ran should win. She did win quite a few races – with another good horse called Zara which won seven races on the trot – so she had quite a good introduction to racing. But it didn't last.

Certain owners want to run horses at certain places, but on lots of occasions it wouldn't be the right place to run the horse. So you have to try and explain. One of the reasons Bryan Jenks was so tremendously successful as an owner was that he left it completely to us. He didn't mind where you ran or when you ran. Of course if you trained for business people, they would probably have business commitments and therefore they didn't want to run the horse when they couldn't go. Then you have a conflict of interests, and it is difficult. But the people who leave you alone and allow you to run where and when you want are obviously going to be more successful than the ones who tie you down to running on certain dates at certain places, where the conditions of the races don't suit them.

We have run horses in races that we'd rather not have run in, that weren't very suitable. But as you get older and get more experienced and a name, you can stand up to the owners and not run where you don't want to. The owners who wanted you to run on certain days – as Fred used to say, 'to train them to board meetings' – were never so successful.

You can't dodge difficult owners by pretending you are out or by not answering the telephone when they ring. That never works. You've always got to face up to things and it's no use trying to hide your head under a stone. It's no use putting things off if you've got a difficult thing to say. If, for example, you've got a good horse and it's got a leg problem you've got to face up to it,

ring the owner and tell him so. It's not a very nice thing to have to do, but you've got to do it one day, so the sooner you do it the better.

Another very good owner, Charlie Hambro of Hambros Bank, paid a lot of money for horses. With the best will in the world we always thought we were buying good horses, but he was an unlucky owner. He had winners, but not the winners that he should have had. His horses seemed to have problems, and through no fault of his. He was one of the nicest owners we ever had and was a very great friend for many years. Unfortunately, the people that you like very much that you most want to have winners quite often don't seem to be very lucky. While you seem to be lucky for somebody you hardly know.

The Carvers wanted to send Trelawny 'chasing, but even though he had schooled brilliantly Fred told them he shouldn't jump fences. I've known Stella Carver all my life since I was six years old. They were difficult owners, and had we told them the horse had jumped fences well, I think they would have wanted to

Guy, aged 17, on his first point-to-point winner, Creola, who subsequently won the Welsh Grand National when ridden by Michael Scudamore. Altogether we won four Welsh Nationals. He was owned by Charlie Nixon, who is holding him and who was an enormous help to us in the early part of our lives. He farmed a lot of land that we used to work over.

83

Scarlett coming in, having won a point-to-point at Chaddesley Corbett in Worcestershire on her good mare, Alice Roe. She's being looked at by our friendly neighbouring farmer, Charlie Nixon.

run him over fences. But Fred felt Trelawny had done almost everything for them: he'd won those big races on the flat, and over hurdles, including winning The Spa hurdle race at Cheltenham as it was called then (the Waterford Crystal now). He was then eleven years old. He was a real hurdle-race horse who stood away from the hurdles a long way, so Fred always visualised that if he ran over fences, he would get into trouble and hurt himself. He had been a wonderful servant to them, and Fred felt that he really didn't want him to go and get killed on a racecourse. So he wouldn't ever run over fences.

It's rather like old Gaye Brief. Lots of people asked me why didn't I run him over fences. Well, he's been a wonderful horse to me. He won me a Champion Hurdle, and sixteen races. I said I was going to retire him at the end of my last season, and his owner agreed. I never even schooled him over a fence, and I wouldn't, because he was good to me and I want to be good to him. I always thought that old horses like Bula should never have

84

run over fences. He was killed over fences. He'd been such a wonderful horse over hurdles it seemed to me such a shame to go on with him and do that.

Trelawny was too old to start and do it, and that's one of the reasons why I never schooled Gaye Brief over a fence. We bought him for Sheikh Ali when we were in Ireland. We knew the family very well because we had had Royal Gaye and Gaye Chance, and Gaye Brief was the younger one. We wanted to buy him very much. We badly wanted the owner of Gaye Chance, John Curtis, to buy him, because Gaye Chance was such a very successful horse, and the Curtises were also, and still are, tremendous friends. But just at that period they didn't feel that they could buy another horse. And John Curtis rather felt that as they had had the one very good one of that family, lightning would never strike twice. Of course, it struck about a dozen times with that particular mare! They also declined because Gaye Chance was still in his prime. So the horse was offered to Sheikh Ali.

We also trained for that interesting ventriloquist, Peter Brough, but unfortunately with no success. Very few people realised that he had anything to do with racing. He never came. We met him in the early '50s when we were on holiday in Majorca. He said he'd like to have a horse. We made a great mistake, because we bought him a young horse that had never run. It had a good pedigree, but it was no good.

We would have been much better off, as we learned in later years, with somebody like him who didn't know a great deal about racing to have bought a horse that had run on the flat and possibly won. You can then go on and get a quick return. This is much better than buying what you think is a nice young Irish horse which you hope will be all right and then it goes wrong, and it isn't.

Really the only thing owners want to have is a winner somewhere – and soon. I think I can say we did pretty well for our owners over the years. We never had more than sixty horses, which you should compare with the results of those much bigger stables. Fred, of course, was the first jumping trainer to win £100,000 in prize money in a season for his owners.

7 *On Famous Horses*

Comedy is a fabulous horse. For a hurdle-race horse he's massive. 17.1h.h. is a massive horse anywhere, but he's so beautifully made. I came up in the showing world, and he would have won any middle-weight hunter class, he was so good-looking. He was certainly the best horse we ever had at Kinnersley. When we bought him as a four-year-old, he'd won two flat races. That was his claim to fame. Because he was so very big, he didn't run as a two-year-old, but he ran as a three-year-old and won. He was by Goldhill, so he was by a sprinter and the flat races he won were six or seven furlongs. As he'd been running over short distances obviously our one idea was to get him settled.

The first time we ever ran him was at Nottingham. Ken White rode him and he won. The next time we ran him we took him to Cheltenham to the National Hunt Meeting and Terry Biddlecombe rode him – Terry didn't ride him at Nottingham because he was injured.

The one thing we had made up our minds about was that the horse wanted to be held up, because he was sprint-bred. The flat races he had won had been over shortish distances, and we were frightened that he wouldn't get the trip. So Terry really distinguished himself that day! I don't know what he'd been doing the night before the Cheltenham race. But to cut a long, sad story short, he went to the front right back at the top of the hill, and got beaten by a neck at the post. Fred was actually furious. Comedy should have won. It was a rubbish horse of no consequence that beat him.

And that I suppose was why Terry didn't ride the horse again. Terry went freelance. The row, if you could call it that – I don't think we've ever had a real row – was over Comedy. Fred was very incensed about the way Terry had ridden him. Everybody rides a bad race and everybody makes mistakes, but that was a shocker.

Even at that stage we thought this was a very good horse, because he had this enormous speed, which of course he got from Goldhill. Compared with our other good young hurdlers, we always thought Comedy would be a very good horse, because he had this wonderful physique. He'd got the substance. Normandy was quite a small horse, and Coral Diver was a nice horse but a bit on the leg. Whereas Comedy really was the pattern of a real show horse. Although he was very big, he was all in proportion. From the word 'Go', he was obviously a very good horse, and he turned out to be the best horse we ever trained. Bill Smith rode him that year, and he had won the Triumph Hurdle for us in 1972 on a horse called Zarib. Terry had won the Triumph Hurdle for us on Coral Diver in 1969.

Comedy had always shown enormous speed at home. He was a freak. He's the only good Goldhill jumper there's ever been, and his dam was of no consequence: she only bred one other winner – it wasn't exactly a winning producing family! We bought him against his breeding, but on his conformation. And because he had won two flat races. He'd got ability to win on the flat and was the most lovely horse to look at.

He was never the best jumper in the world, because he was so big, but because he was such a big horse he could get away with it. If he made an error it didn't make much difference to him. He was such a giant of a horse, he could get away with kicking a few hurdles out of the ground. Admittedly, Nottingham where he had won was a completely different thing to a Novices at the National Hunt Meeting, but he'd won terribly impressively. Possibly the flat track at Nottingham suited him.

He jumped quite well for Terry at Cheltenham but he virtually ran away with him. Terry knew the one thing he was supposed to do was settle the horse. But he didn't give the horse the chance to settle. Over the years everybody makes mistakes: the best jockey in the world, the best trainer in the world, we all do these silly things we regret afterwards. That was just one of the things that happen in racing.

Speed was Comedy's great thing, so at home we always tried to work him behind other horses to make him settle. Which, in the end of course, he'd got to do. Most horses do, and with age he settled more and more and consequently became an easier ride. Probably Terry had the worst of him when he rode him at Cheltenham – which at the time we perhaps overlooked. And he

tended to jump to the right which again was no help at Cheltenham. When Ken White rode him at Nottingham – it's a very level left-handed track – he was always apt to jump slightly to the right, which was unfortunate. But he was a very, very good horse. He won three Fighting Fifth Hurdles at Newcastle which is why they now have a Comedy of Errors Hurdle Race.

Cheltenham wasn't really his track. Being by a sprinter you would have wondered whether he really got the trip up the hill. And I always wondered if he really came *down* the hill because he was such a massive horse, that you'd think he'd be much better off on a level flat track. Yet he won two Champion Hurdles in 1973 and 1975 and was second in the one in between. He met Sea Pigeon three times and beat him twice and Sea Pigeon was a very, very good horse.

Comedy was one of the best Champion Hurdle racehorses I've seen over the years, and not particularly because we trained him. He proved it really because it's not often a horse wins a race like the Champion, get beaten the following year and then comes out

OPPOSITE
Nicolaus Silver being led in by his owner, Jeremy Vaughan, after winning the 1961 National. My son, Guy, is on the right.

ABOVE
After the National with the winning rider, Bobby Beasley. This photograph was taken at Kinnersley. Nicolaus Silver, bought by us at Goffs for 2,500 guineas, was almost a show-horse in looks. The editor of this book was underbidder to us!

and wins again. It's most unusual. They always say they never come back. I think he's the only one to have done so. That proves what a good horse he was.

In the 1974 Champion, the one that he lost, Fred and I weren't all that happy with Bill Smith's riding. We felt he should have won, though Bill Smith said, I believe, that 'the horse wasn't himself'.

At the time we did rather blame the rider. But it's such an easy thing to do: to blame your rider. We had no reason to believe there was anything wrong with the horse. We had all sorts of tests done: there was nothing wrong with him. He went on that season and won after that.

We just thought that Bill Smith didn't ride a very intelligent race. But we all make mistakes. People said he was caught napping. Well, I think he played into Lanzarote's hands. Comedy had got enormous speed but he didn't ride him to use it. Pitman rode him out of it that time. I can't think how he managed to do it! But he did. We never got within striking distance of Lanzarote when he went on going down the hill.

Fred thought Smith gave him too much leeway. Fred always said that at Cheltenham, when you went past the Water, you always wanted to be within striking distance of what you thought was your danger. We thought he was about ten or twelve lengths behind Lanzarote at that period. He shouldn't have been that far behind. Pitman literally stole a march on him and he got first run down the hill. Comedy, being a very massive horse, didn't come down the hill that well anyway, and Pitman had really won his race at the second last. That was the biggest disappointment we ever had.

1975, when he won again, was a marvellous year, because they don't usually come back. He and Sea Pigeon are about the only two. Sea Pigeon hadn't won it, but he'd run in a couple of Champions in 1978 and '79 before he won it in 1980 and they don't often do that either.

The other Champion Hurdle we thought we ought to have won was Spartan General's in 1965. Terry thought so too: he even said so in his book. It's all long gone now, but Spartan General should have won it: he was a better horse than the winner, that 50 to 1 shot Kirriemuir.

We ran Comedy once over fences at Worcester, not because the owners wanted it. They were marvellous owners. It was us. We thought that as he's a great big horse, he'd jump fences. But he never really jumped fences. We ran him at Worcester because the fences are very easy. John Burke rode him. He'd ridden him to win some hurdle races, so he knew the horse. But Comedy didn't really bend his back. He *launched* himself at the fences. We had a horror that something would happen to him like those good horses: like Bula breaking his shoulder and Lanzarote breaking his leg over fences.

Comedy had been a wonderful horse to us and we didn't want anything horrible to happen to him. I may be silly and it may sound sentimental – I suppose in racing you shouldn't be sentimental – but we were lucky in the fact that he was owned by somebody who was as equally sentimental as we were. It was the first horse that Ted Wheatley had ever owned. When Fred suggested retiring him, not running him over fences and not running him in mediocre hurdle races after he'd been Champion, he agreed. So he retired when he was ten. I had him as my hack for ten lovely years, so obviously he's my favourite. I know you shouldn't be sentimental in racing, but that's how it turned out with Comedy. He made a lot of people very happy. And he led a lovely life himself.

It was my mother, once again looking for a show horse, who found E.S.B. She saw him as an unbroken three-year-old and she loved him. But he was slightly pigeon-toed, which would have ruled him out for showing. So she rang up and said, 'I've seen a lovely horse and I believe he's got a good racing pedigree. You should go and see him.'

We did and we bought him. Funnily enough he was in a field next door to where Stella Carver lived. She'd been looking at him over the fence for two years, and had never realised that he was such a nice horse. We bought him for Rolie Oliver who was the father of Michael Oliver the trainer, quite nearby, who won the Grand National with West Tip.

The first time we ever fancied E.S.B. we took him as a three-year-old to Wincanton on Boxing Day and put a boy called Titch Humphries on him. And he won. The Olivers won a fortune for they were inveterate gamblers. But we decided he wasn't really a hurdle-race horse. In those days they used to have a four-year-old Juvenile Chase at Cheltenham's National Hunt Meeting. We decided that was the race we'd like to win with him. Martin Molony was then in his heyday, so we got Martin over from

91

A good action shot of Terry Biddlecombe winning the Gold Cup on Woodland Venture jumping the last fence with Stan Mellor on Stalbridge Colonist who was second.

Ireland to ride E.S.B. at Birmingham, to give the horse a bit of experience. We wanted him to give the horse a quiet race, because we didn't want to collect any penalties by winning (in those days you got penalties for everything). He finished sixth at Birmingham and I can always remember Martin saying when he got off, 'I couldn't have been any nearer', much to Fred's fury.

Anyway, we decided to press on with our objective, the Juvenile Chase. We didn't run him again before Cheltenham. In those days Captain Cyril Harty, Eddie Harty's father, was Martin Molony's mentor. So Fred said to Cyril, 'Martin must catch hold of this horse and really give him a ride if he's going to win this!'

Cyril Harty said, 'Jasus, Fred! *You* tell him.'

We went into the paddock and Fred said to Martin, 'Catch hold of him. Give him a ride. Don't go to sleep on him like you did at Birmingham.' He jumped out of the gate in that four-year-old chase, made all the running and won by twenty lengths. That was E.S.B.'s beginning.

We lost the horse for a time when the Carvers were training him themselves. Rolie Oliver, who owned him first, got into trouble gambling, so the horse had to be sold to raise the money. We decided the best thing we could do was to offer him to Geoffrey

Kohn, who subsequently owned Sundew who won the National. We knew Geoffrey well: his wife Dora has been a friend for some years. So Fred offered E.S.B. to Geoffrey.

He, unbeknown to us, immediately rang up Leonard Carver and said Fred had offered him this horse. Leonard said 'I'll take half of him.' So he was a partnership horse between Geoffrey Kohn and Leonard Carver. It was an acrimonious partnership because each wanted the horse to run in their name. In those days you could alternate entries, running a horse in, say, Mrs Stella Carver's name at Worcester this week and in Mrs Geoffrey Kohn's next week at Cheltenham. But the actual races don't come out like that. You made a plan to run the horse in one race which then turned out to be unsuitable. So you'd miss a couple of races, and then the horse would be running in two races in Kohn's name and none in Carver's name.

They decided E.S.B. should be sold to dissolve the unhappy partnership and sent him up to Newmarket to be sold under the hammer. But neither partner would tell Fred whether they were interested in buying him. The horse was knocked down to Leonard Carver for the huge sum in those days of 9,000 guineas. So he bought Kohn out. Kohn at the time also owned Royal Serenade, a good flat race horse who was sold at the same sale to go to America, and made a very, very good stallion. Even he only fetched the same amount of money initially as E.S.B., though he was syndicated in later years for fortunes.

Leonard had E.S.B. home and decided to train him himself. And this was really the best thing that could have happened to us! Syd Mercer had him to start with and then Leonard had him at home. They ran him lots of times but he won only one small race so, of course, he went down and down in the handicap. After about a season and a half of this, Stella's father, an old chap we'd known for years, by the name of Pearce, a butcher from Birmingham, got hold of Stella. He apparently said to her, 'Why don't you send the horse back to somebody who knows something about him? Send him back to Fred.'

The horse came back to us and by then he was only getting 10st 7lb in quite decent races. He won six races on the trot that season. Then Leonard rang up and said, 'I'm going to Switzerland for a fortnight's skiing. Don't run my horse while I'm away. But have him ready to win at Manchester when I come back.' Which we did and he did.

Then he went on and he won the National in the year that Devon Loch had his disaster. Fred always maintained that we would have been an unlucky loser, because you can see from the film that the horse Jack Dowdeswell rode brought us literally to a halt at Valentine's. We must have lost ten lengths. But that's the swings and roundabouts of the National. We did get back on terms again at the last, but by then Devon Loch was going away from us. Fred always thought that a horse was like a long-distance runner, and that the Queen Mother's Devon Loch just ran out of oxygen, like you see in marathon runners. We've always thought that.

E.S.B. went on and won many good races after the National, including the Sefton. The year in which he won the National and six races, he went on and got beaten a head in what became The Whitbread Gold Cup, then a top class race run at old Hurst Park, and called ironically the Queen Elizabeth Chase.

As E.S.B. was jumping the last fence in the National, Fred and I turned to each other and said, 'Oh, he's second. He's run a super race.' Then this terrible thing happened to Devon Loch and Fred shouted, 'Good God! What a terrible thing!' Then the next second, he said, 'Well, we've won a National. I can't believe it. And what a way to win it.' With that, he sort of hurtled down the steps and so did I. It really took all the pleasure from it.

After the race Fred tried to sympathise with the Queen Mother. But she said, 'No, Mr Rimell, you won the National. And that is it.' She was marvellous, absolutely marvellous. Fred met her quite a number of times. He used to go to those dinners that Whitbread give at their Brewery. The Queen Mother was always there. Then a couple of times we went to Garden Parties at the Palace, when you can select which member of the Royal Family you'd like to meet. You ask the Gentlemen at Arms, saying whom you'd like to meet and Fred always wanted to talk to the Queen Mother.

E.S.B. had a marvellous life. The Carvers had a beautiful park at their home at Lapworth, and the horse was pensioned-off there. He lived, I think, to the age of thirty odd, and was very well looked after.

The least nice owner we ever trained for was Teazy-Weazy Raymond, the hairdresser. We didn't 'find' him as an owner. He bought Rag Trade at public auction at Doncaster to win a National. I don't know who trained him that season – but he bought him in the February and ran him in the National at the end of March.

The next thing was, Teazy-Weazy rang up Fred and said would he train him for the following year's National? Fred said he would. He had ridden for Teazy-Weazy before the war, so he knew him. He was sent to us specifically, I suppose, because we had a very good National record.

Rag Trade looked a clumsy horse and he was a clumsy horse. But he had got quite a lot of ability because he won a Welsh National the same year that he won the Grand National and he galloped through about three fences in that, but still was good enough to win it. So he was a fully exposed horse when he went for the Grand National: he had his maximum weight. There was no question of him having a few runs down the track or anything like that, he was fully exposed. And John Burke was a good enough horseman to manage him. He beat Red Rum.

Whether Teazy-Weazy gambled, I don't know. I have no idea what he did. I just know that he was a man that I didn't personally like. He didn't really appreciate the fact that you had won the National for him. I just think he thought we should win it anyway. He had won it previously with a horse, Ayala, trained by Keith Piggot. So this was his second National winner anyway. He

My son-in-law, Robin Knipe, a leading amateur, winning at Kempton Park on The Fossa. This horse later won the Scottish Grand National.

was not very generous about presents to the lads and the jockey.

We had four National winners, but Nicolaus Silver was the one horse we thought would win. Jeremy Vaughan who owned him, was away in Spain five or six days before the National. Fred sent him a telegram saying the horse had done a wonderful gallop. He had previously run at Cheltenham at the big meeting and had won the Kim Muir ridden by a very nice man and good amateur, Bill Tellwright, who got killed schooling at home in the mid 1980s.

Nicolaus Silver had only one serious gallop between the Kim Muir and the National, but he did a marvellous piece of work. Fred sent Jeremy a cable saying 'HORSE PUT UP WONDERFUL GALLOP, HAS A VERY, VERY GOOD CHANCE'. Jeremy won a fortune over him. He backed him from forty to one down to twenty-eight to one. That was one of Jeremy's 'Good Things'!

We always said our first proper National winner was Nicolaus Silver and we had more pleasure from that National than from any of our others. He was owned by somebody we knew very well, and he was a beautiful horse, and a precision jumper. In Ireland he wasn't thought a great deal of, because they never realised that Nicolaus Silver was a top-of-the-ground horse. He was a stone better horse on good ground.

The year after he won the National in 1961 he ran again when Kilmore won it, and I always thought that had the ground been right in 1962 he'd have won another one. It was very heavy. He couldn't act in it at all. He hated it. He was a beautiful-actioned horse, a show horse, and that's what really defeated him. Unfortunately, his owner got into money problems and he had to be sold, which was a tragedy.

He was only beaten a head in the Whitbread by Pas Seul, who won a Cheltenham Gold Cup and that was on the ground he loved. Then he was bought by Bernard Sunley. He went back to the Sunleys and I think the horse broke his leg out hunting, really rather a tragedy.

Woodland Venture being led in after winning the Gold Cup by his owner and breeder, Harry Collins, who was a farmer down in Dorset. He was a friend and neighbour of the Dufosees, who introduced him to us, but whom he beat in this race!

We just hoped that Woodland Venture would run well in his Gold Cup in 1967. He wasn't what you'd call a live contender, but he wasn't a complete outsider. He was inexperienced, never a very good jumper, and an ignorant horse. But Terry always had quite a feeling for Woodland Venture. In spite of the horse giving him a couple of frightful falls, he was still prepared to ride him, so he always thought the horse had ability.

The year he won the Gold Cup he beat Stalbridge Colonist. That

The most lovely picture of Terry about to take his tack off after winning the Gold Cup on Woodland Venture.

was very satisfactory for Harry Collins because the Dufossees were his next-door West Country neighbours and it had been the Dufossees who first suggested that Harry Collins send the horse to Fred. Of course, they were quite certain that their Stalbridge Colonist was going to beat Harry, so it was a good bit of a very friendly needle match. The Dufossees were very disappointed that they didn't win. But Harry was triumphant. It gave us an enormous amount of satisfaction to win a race for somebody like that because he had bred the horse. He didn't go out and buy it. He had it all its life. He was a great man to train for and he still is a very great friend.

After his Gold Cup, Woodland Venture fell in the King George at Kempton. He would have won that. From then on he didn't ever seem to sparkle. He went back to Harry Collins, who had moved to Norfolk where he ran a lot of sheep. The horse went back to him in the summer, and caught Black's Disease, which you get from sheep apparently, and the horse died up there.

Both our Gold Cup winners were young and relatively inexperienced, and I can't say that during the season they really made us feel that they were Gold Cup horses. We started to hope when Royal Frolic won the Greenall Whitley, which was a good race that year – it usually is a hard race to win. He only had 10st 6lb on him, but he won it very impressively.

But the main reason he was entered in the Gold Cup was the fact that we knew his owner Sir Edward Hanmer was very, very ill and didn't have long to go. We thought, 'Wouldn't it be wonderful if we could win the Gold Cup for him?' We didn't think that he would ever live to see him run the following year. Had he belonged to somebody else he possibly wouldn't have run in it.

Old Sir Edward, we were pretty sure, was dying. We'd had connections with him since 1936. He was always a bit of a martinet. But Fred rang him up, 'Sir Edward, I'd like to run Royal Frolic in the Gold Cup.'

There was a bit of a silence and then Sir Edward said, 'Don't you think it's a year too soon?'

Fred, who was always quite quick on the uptake said, 'Sir Edward, don't you think we're running out of time?'

There was a sort of chuckle and he said, 'I think perhaps you're right. You go ahead and run it if you want to.' He did in fact die six weeks later.

Both Fred and I always thought that Gay Trip should have won his second National in 1972. The film shows that he was on the outside all the way from going to Becher's second time. He must have given lengths and lengths away – very much more lost ground than the distance he was beaten by. I think that Terry in his heart thought so too. He just had one of his off-days, that day. I think he'd had one of his nights out. There's no doubt about it: Gay Trip should have won. He was giving a lot of weight away to Well To Do, but he was quite capable of giving it away, had he not been asked to give about thirty lengths away.

He was bought through Pat Taaffe which is why Pat rode him in the 1970 National which he won. Fred happened to see Pat at some dinner in London and said he was looking for a nice horse. Pat said, 'If I ever hear of one, I'll give you a ring.' He rang up and said he knew this horse. We went over to Ireland and saw him out in a field and with a blister on his leg! We said, 'We like him but we can't do anything about it until the blister comes off.'

We had to wait a month until it healed. Then we went over again, saw him, and loved him. He was Fred's sort of horse and my sort of horse. He was just 16 h.h., not a massive big horse. He'd won a hurdle race, so obviously we were buying him as a chaser because he wasn't a novice over hurdles.

We bought him for a very great friend of ours, Anthony Chambers, who was Joint Master of our local hounds, the Croome, and who had ridden five winners under National Hunt rules himself. The first time we ran him was at Newbury in a novice chase. We thought he'd win, but he fell at the Water. The next time he ran he went to Doncaster and won. From then on he never looked back. He was the most super jumper. Not being too big, he could shorten his stride or lengthen his stride.

Pat Taaffe rode him in the National because Terry was smashed up and we were hunting round for a National jockey, when suddenly we said, 'What about Pat Taaffe? He found the horse for us. So let's ask him.' We rang him up and he said, 'Yes, I'd love to ride.' He'd never ridden him in a race before. But he was a class horse and class horses in those days usually won Nationals in the end.

Since then people have used him as an example of the classy two-miler who can win a National. People say, 'So-and-so is a real Gay Trip type . . .' because he never won a three mile race and yet could stay 4½ miles at Liverpool. Gay Trip won two Mackesons and numerous two, or two-and-a-half mile races, but he never won a three mile chase . . .

Before his National in 1970, we thought he was a very athletic little horse. He was a real athlete and, although he fell the first time out for us he was a very good jumper. We always thought that E.S.B. didn't stay – he was really a two-and-a-half mile horse and he never did stay properly although he won the National. I don't think Gay Trip stayed, but he'd got that bit of class about him, and in those days the fences weren't modified. It was a much harder task to win a National then. Jumping was the name of the game. Today you've got to have a horse that stays a lot better, because the fences are that much easier, so it's more of a race. Years ago it was a jumping competition. That's the way I look at it. Today your moderate two-and-a-half mile horse wouldn't have the speed. I'm sure I'm right about that.

Coral Diver was a very good horse when he won the Triumph Hurdle in 1969 and he's one of the few Triumph Hurdle winners that subsequently went on and won very good races after. He won the Scottish Champion Hurdle, and a Welsh Champion. He was fourth in a Champion Hurdle. He won a lot of races, and was a very good horse.

He just lacked top-class ability: he wasn't quite good enough to win a Champion though we always thought when he had won the Triumph that he would go on and be a Champion Hurdle race horse.

We made a mistake. He was a colt when he won the Triumph and we thought that he would go on and possibly develop into a good chaser, and so we had him gelded. In hindsight we shouldn't have done. Had we left him as a colt we might have won the Champion Hurdle with him the following year. It seemed to take that bit of sparkle away from him and he wasn't a colty horse either. If we'd left him . . . but there you are. We thought we were doing the right thing. We thought colts didn't last as jumpers. We should have left him as a colt, and he would probably have gone on and made a good National Hunt stallion.

Normandy remained a colt. He was the same age, but he wasn't big enough for a chaser. He was about 15.3 h.h., but he hadn't got the bone or physique in anyway that Coral Diver had. He was a lovely pattern of a horse, but he wasn't a big horse. He subsequently went on as a stallion.

I wasn't there at Leopardstown the day he beat Persian War in the Irish Sweeps. I was going over with Bryan Jenks. We had got runners in England on the Boxing Day at Wolverhampton – sounds inspiring! Fred had gone over when the horse went. I was going over with Bryan Jenks to fly from Birmingham. And it was thick fog, so we couldn't take off. So the best we could do was listen to the race on the radio and to watch it on a little tiny monitor at Wolverhampton racecourse.

Normandy was a super horse, and one of my favourites, because I forced Bryan to buy him. Robert Sangster had said he wouldn't buy him, and Bryan said at first that he'd got a very good one of the same age in Coral Diver. Anyway, we talked Bryan into buying it. So I badly wanted to go over when he ran in the Irish Sweeps, but it wasn't to be because of the fog. I'm sure it was one of the best races Terry ever rode in his life. It was as good a race as the bad race he rode on Gay Trip in the National, when he got beaten. So I suppose one counteracts the other. Terry undoubtedly won the Irish Sweeps for us.

And after the race, Persian War's owner, that man Alper, objected to the first two! Never heard such nonsense! Terry had always got the inside anyway, and Alper had absolutely nothing to object about. From Fred's description, Terry seemed to be inspired that day.

We never ran Normandy over fences because, though he was a brilliant jumper, he was small. In this day and age, we would probably have run him over fences. He was the only bad-tempered horse we ever had at Kinnersley and being a colt and bad-tempered made life difficult. We always thought he'd make a good stallion, but he didn't seem to. Perhaps he didn't have the right mares, but at stud was never a roaring success.

Honour Bound was a colt, too. He won the Waterford Crystal at Cheltenham, then the Martin Mahoney at Punchestown the same season, and that same summer won the Yorkshire Cup at Doncaster with Doug Smith riding. He turned out to be a top N.H. sire and sired Tied Cottage who was first past the post in the Cheltenham Gold Cup in 1980.

Gaye Brief was the last horse Fred bought. We gave £20,000 for him as a four-year-old, which by today's standards is peanuts. Even before he ran we knew he could definitely go. He was my first runner for Sheikh Ali so I wanted to win. We ran him at Hereford and he won by about four lengths. That first season he won four races, and because I didn't think he'd be ready for the hurly-burly of Cheltenham I ran him at Chepstow in the Players' Final, which he won. The next year he won the Champion Hurdle as a six-year-old, and made me the first woman to train a Champion Hurdler.

The last race he ever ran was at Newton Abbot. It was always the intention that my granddaughter Katie should ride him and she finished second in a three mile two furlong hurdle. Sheikh Ali gave him to me to retire in May 1989, and I can now see him every day, grazing with Comedy in a field below my house. I may say he retired completely sound without a blemish on him.

On Buying   8

I don't like big horses: there are far too many problems with them. If you don't have a wind problem, you usually have a leg problem. The ideal size for me is 16h.h. to 16.1h.h. I'm sure you should never breed from an enormous big mare. Years ago Ruby Holland-Martin from the Overbury Stud, who was one of the most successful breeders and was a friend of Fred's, said, 'Never have a brood mare over 16 hands.' I'm absolutely certain he was right. You breed a giant, and as soon as you breed a giant you have problems. Yet I can defeat my own argument: the best horse we ever had at Kinnersley was Comedy of Errors who is in fact 17.1 hands. But he is so beautifully made: he has such depth, and short legs. He is all correct. So you can have some big horses –there is an exception to every rule.

Neither Fred nor I had a particular interest for any particular stallion. Deep Run has never been enormously successful for us. And we never had a winner by Spartan General, whom we trained for the whole of his jumping career. We hardly had any Spartan General horses, which seems very odd, because he had a tremendous lot of winners, but not for us.

Spartan Generals always took a long time to come to themselves, of course. But he was a good horse himself, very courageous. He was second in the Champion Hurdle. Terry always says that he ought to have won it on him. And he was one of the few colts to go on and win over fences.

When I'm off to the sales looking for three- and four-year-olds, I believe conformation is most important. You start at the bottom and work up. The first and foremost thing is that you've got to have good forelegs. You don't like something that's got long pasterns, or very short pasterns; they've got to be correct. You don't want something that's back of its knees or upright in front.

And you work up from there. It wants to have a good shoulder.

It is vital to have a lovely sloping shoulder and not an upright one. You want a horse with a nice intelligent head. It never bothers me, and it never has done, if a horse has curby hocks. Gay Trip had the most frightful curby hocks, and he won two Mackesons, a Grand National, and was second in the National, so they wouldn't bother me!

I like a nice, fine, intelligent head, but not a feminine head, in other words not an 'Araby' head. Although a very good horse we had, Connaught Ranger who won the Triumph Hurdle and lots of other races, had the most feminine Araby head you've ever seen. But he had been a very difficult horse before he came to us from France, where Lord Derby had him in training. In fact, after he'd won the Triumph Hurdle, Lord Derby said to Fred, 'I can't think how you've done it, Fred, because we couldn't even get him out of the yard in France!'

You want big ears, and a good bold eye. I hate small ears. For the girth, you want to have some depth. You don't want something that you can drive a bus underneath.

It doesn't matter how they trot, but they've got to walk really well. As Tom Cooper will tell you – and he's probably the best judge of a racehorse in the world – 'racehorses aren't made to trot. See them walk and gallop.' I'm sure he's right. You want a really good swinging walk. You need to look at them both crossing you and from behind, both ways. It's essential to see them walk when you go to the yearling sales, very few people will even ask to see them trot. They only want to see them walk, which is correct. Horses with massive bodies simply weren't designed to carry those enormous bodies at speed. Comedy's body was so beauti-fully in proportion he's never looked a big horse, whereas Rag Trade looked like a big Suffolk Punch. You're much better to have 16 hands with quality.

On the pedigree side we always liked to have a good dam. A winner perhaps, but certainly the dam of winners, like Artiste Gaye who produced Gaye Brief, Royal Gaye and Gaye Chance. She had eleven foals and ten of them won. Now if you get a dam like that, the offspring will win whatever the sire. Artiste Gaye was unbroken and it may be a good thing to have a dam that hasn't done any racing. If you get a good winning family on the dam's side, you'll be jolly unlucky if you don't get a winner.

You really want both a good dam plus conformation. The breeding element in the case of the dam is very important.

Lester Piggott winning the Great Metropolitan at Epsom on a horse of our leading owner, Bryan Jenks, called Pick Me Up trained by Fred. Lester was always a racing hero to Fred and me.

Breeding has quite a lot to do with success, but conformation more so. I was brought up in the showing world, so therefore I've always been keen on conformation.

I don't like chestnuts. We never did. I don't know why, because there have been plenty of good chestnut horses. We had a very good horse called Red Thorn who was a chestnut, who won the Sefton and was subsequently killed in the Great Yorkshire where he broke a leg. One always went for a nice bay or brown horse, but I've never been put off by black horses after having had Unconditional Surrender, who was well named by Frank Jordison as he was by Flag of Truce out of Scotch Widow. A lot of people are put off by black horses but Fred always used to say, 'You never see a good horse a bad colour.' I'm sure that's true. The question of colour may have cost us a few horses.

When you go to Ireland you win some and you lose some. We could have bought a good horse called Klaxton, but we didn't and Bob Turnell bought him. We ought to have bought him, but we didn't.

As to age, one wouldn't have gone out and bought The Fossa, but he was sent to us. You'd have thought we wouldn't have much chance of winning anything much with him, because when he came to us he'd run nineteen times the season before and hadn't won! So he'd had an awful lot of racing and was very much a second-hand article. But he was a marvellous horse and the most wonderful jumper. He won the Sefton, the Scottish National with Andrew Turnell and he ran in the National the year that Foinavon brought everything down. We always thought that he would have won, but then you always think you're going to win the National! The following year he ran again in the National, finished well, and was subsequently sold to Andrew Parker Bowles to ride in the Grand Military.

If one had trained him earlier in his career he would have been a very good horse, but he had had so much racing that the poor thing was a bit fed up with it. He thrived on little work and plenty to eat, which I think he probably hadn't had before! We wouldn't have gone out and bought him at that age and with that background, but he was sent to us to train, and things turned out right.

We wouldn't have bought Deep Run. John Magnier of the Coolmore stud in Tipperary, bought him. He'd been a good two-year-old, but was not good as a three-year-old, and after John

Magnier bought him at the December Sales, he rang up and said to Fred, 'I'm sending you a colt. I want you to win a hurdle race with him, because I want to make him into a dual-purpose stallion.'

He duly won, when Tommy Stack rode him at Doncaster. He was due to run again when John Magnier rang up from Ireland and said, 'Ship the horse at once! Wrekin Rambler has died. Deep Run's got to cover all his mares.' So he went straight out of training in February and covered all Wrekin Rambler's mares and he never looked back.

He covered a fantastic number of mares. He wasn't a very big horse, and he was a very poor mover. He couldn't trot. And yet he was the most successful N.H. stallion that I can remember. I think John Magnier picked him out because they were terribly keen on his sire Pampered King, and possibly because he was a very good two-year-old. As a three-year-old he could have got stumped up on the firm ground. He had a very good make and shape, but he just wasn't frightfully big, though obviously big enough.

One of the good horses I missed was Jimmy FitzGerald's Forgive 'N Forget who won the Gold Cup. He belonged first to Barney Curley, and was trained by Brennan on the Curragh. I tried very hard to buy him, and made an offer for him. But they wouldn't accept it. I subsequently upped my offer to what they had asked for him, but they still said 'No'. Then they sold him to FitzGerald. I know they sold him for exactly the same price I'd offered. So I didn't get him, and he went and won the Gold Cup! There you are: you win some and you lose some.

Fred Winter, I believe, had tried to buy Gay Trip and then turned him down because he thought he wasn't big enough. Then we went in, bought him and won a National with him. Swings and roundabouts . . . all trainers can tell you these things.

Finding young horses out in the field is probably the best in the long run. You have spells when you think it's marvellous to buy some ex-flat racehorse at Newmarket with good form. But they very seldom go on to make good jumpers. They don't last. One of the few horses we ever bought from Newmarket Sales who went on was Jupiter Boy, who won us a Mackeson. (We won four Mackesons.) Jupiter Boy used to be trained on the flat by Charlie Nelson, and he was one of the few ex-flat horses that went on to make a very good chaser. By and large half the purchasing of horses is luck!

Terry winning at Sandown on Domacorn who was subsequently second in the Gold Cup.

We hardly ever bought a horse without having got an order to buy one. You'd get various people who would say, 'Buy me a nice chaser.' But it's a very difficult thing to go out and buy a chaser ready-made, and it's usually very expensive. So you've got to make your chasers. We went through a spell when we used to buy a lot of three-year-olds from Newmarket and we won three Triumph Hurdles, so that was quite successful.

We didn't have owners with bottomless pockets. People thought that Sheikh Ali being an Arab must have been enormously rich. But Sheikh Ali never in his life gave a big price for a horse with us. Gaye Brief cost £20,000, which isn't the earth nowadays for jumpers. I don't know what Fred Winter gave for horses for Sheikh Ali, but *we* never gave big prices for his horses. At the going rate, Gaye Brief was very cheap. Gaye Chance was bought at auction, for 10,000 guineas under the hammer, several years ago.

Gaye Chance and Royal Gaye had made the family very successful and we'd known Phil Sweeney, who had the family, ever since 1946. We trained one for him over here, but it wasn't a great deal of good. We always remained friendly with him and we used to go back looking at his horses in Ireland. We bought Royal Gaye off him unbroken in a field. He wasn't expensive and he was very successful, so we were obviously keen to buy Gaye Chance. Then we were equally keen to buy Gaye Brief because it had been such a successful family, a wonderful family for us. I've still got the last but one, called Gaye Memory, and I've run her in bumper races and she's won two and she's now in foal, so I've still got part of the family.

We went over to Ireland once with Bryan Jenks and Robert Sangster and we looked at Normandy. We liked him very much, but Robert said, 'I don't want to buy a four-year-old colt. I want to buy a chaser.'

So Fred turned to Bryan and said, 'Bryan, you'll have to have him.'

Bryan said, 'All right, I will.'

So that's how he bought Normandy, one of our most successful horses for Bryan, though we really went to buy it for Robert. Instead we bought a horse for Robert Sangster called Sunny Lad who eventually won Robert the Topham Trophy, so that was quite a successful buy, too. He'd wanted a chaser: he got one who won at Liverpool.

Gay Trip being paraded through Upton after his National win in 1970. He is being led by 'Bromyard' (Frank Pullen) who did him. On the right is Fred.

In those days Jack Doyle used to be our spotter in Ireland and it was a very successful partnership which worked for years. Jack Doyle pretty well spotted all of our horses for us, and then Fred or I, or both of us, used to go over and buy them. But it was really through Jack Doyle that most of those good horses were purchased. Then in the later years, Jack turned to the flat racing side, buying yearlings. He doesn't really get involved in jumpers now. He's got older, and doesn't scoot about the country looking at jumpers like he used to do in the old days. So that alliance ceased.

We never bought horses in France as, for example, Ryan Price used to. We always had the problem that neither of us spoke French! We were always keen on Ireland. We once tried to buy a horse in France called Pitpan, who's now quite a successful stallion, but he didn't pass our vet: he used to burst blood vessels. About a month later, Fulke Walwyn went over, and bought him, and they got him past their vet. Over in England, trained by Fulke, he won one race only, but that was at Windsor, and he beat

Sir Edward Hanmer's Royal Mark winning the Wedding Day Chase on the very day that Princess Anne married Captain Mark Phillips!

a horse of ours, Hilltop. But that was the only race Pitpan ever won in England.

We've always liked Ireland from the old days when the Hartys were very much involved with us. 'Buster' Harty originally came over to us, followed closely by Eddie Harty, who is now a bloodstock agent. Buster rode for us very successfully as an amateur and Eddie rode Glenn when he won the Welsh National and also Jupiter Boy when he won the Mackeson. We bought a lot of horses through the Hartys over the years and then we got involved with Jack Doyle, who seemed to suit everybody very well. He's a very likeable character and like Cyril Harty, a very good judge.

If you've got an agent you want to stick with him, particularly somebody like Doyle, who lived in Ireland, and in those days was very active going round all the meetings. He'd see a horse and he'd ring you up straight away. And if you were in the happy position – which in those days we were – of having several rich owners in the yard, Doyle could tell you all about a horse, and Fred and I would go over and see it, knowing we'd got a buyer. We were in a fortunate position.

112

Nowadays there's far more money in breeding for N.H. racing than there used to be. Years ago nobody wanted a filly, anyway. Now you get the 5lb allowance for fillies. It's made the world of difference. The first filly to put N.H. racing on the map was Kirsten followed by Glencarrig Lady winning the Gold Cup, and Dawn Run, who certainly made a greater impact than any other filly that I can remember. Dawn Run was a fantastic mare. You've got to go back to Bramble Tudor before Glencarrig Lady – that's lifetimes ago. We had no outstanding mares because in those days we didn't go to buy fillies, which was possibly a mistake. When I was training I had one really good filly, called Nassau Royale, but unfortunately she was killed at Ascot.

Fred wasn't really prejudiced against fillies; he just wasn't mad about them. It's an old-fashioned idea, and maybe we hadn't moved with the times sufficiently. Now there are all sorts of incentives, apart from the allowance: you have a lot of fillies' races which are quite valuable, Tattersalls run a series of chases, and there's a series of races for hurdle race fillies. So if you've got a good filly you can win a lot of money.

I bought a brood mare before a dispersal sale from Lord McAlpine who had Dobsons Stud. I happened to send two of my other brood mares down there to be covered by Tremblant, who belonged to Khaled Abdullah in his racing days and who had won the Cambridgeshire with 9st 8lb. I'd never seen him in the flesh, but I'd loved him on the television and always thought he was a most courageous horse. He was standing near Henley-on-Thames, so I sent my two treasures down there and the stud groom rang me up and said, 'Mrs Rimell, I think you should come and look at your foal. I'm not sure about its front legs.'

So I went speeding off down, because I'd never seen the horse in the flesh. I didn't think there was anything wrong with the foal, but I was very grateful for the stud groom's interest, and obviously gave him a drink, because I thought he'd looked after me rather well. About a week later he rang up and said, 'We're having a dispersal sale. Would you like to buy a grey mare we've got? She's a jumping mare, so I don't think she'd be interesting to anyone else in this establishment, but she might be to you.'

I knew the mare quite well because I remember beating her at Ascot with another three-year-old. She'd won over hurdles and she'd won on the flat and she was tested in foal to Tremblant, and I bought her for, I thought, a very reasonable figure. And I now have a very nice colt foal out of her. So maybe she will help keep me in my old age!

I think all stallions should have at least a 100+ Timeform rating, and they should not have any hereditary complaint. They should all be licensed. I believe this very strongly. I said so at the Thoroughbred Breeders' Association meeting I went to. I don't think that a horse which had a wind problem should be allowed to stand. It shouldn't have a licence. People who are prepared to put their horses up for inspection to receive a licence should then be allowed to advertise them as such. And the ones that aren't prepared to, just wouldn't get a licence and couldn't advertise. It's done quite successfully with the H.I.S. – they have them inspected by a veterinary group; the same thing should be done for N.H. stallions.

I had quite a lot of support from the T.B.A. I'm perfectly sure that so many things are hereditary and that the mare is responsible for seventy per cent of whatever is inherited. People who have a mare and run it and it doesn't prove successful then say 'We'll breed from it.' That is a mistake. Get rid of it. Only breed from something that's good or from a good family. And also only breed from a *sound* family, on both sides. Don't pick up the catalogue and see that the mare 'retired to stud as a four-year-old "owing to an accident".' It'll have a bowed tendon or something like that.

The sort of winning distance I look for in the catalogue when I'm buying foals or yearlings ought to be that of a sire that's won from anything over a mile. Today you get so many horses winning that are by sprinters. But horses that are labelled sprinters would probably get a longer distance just as well if they ran over it.

I've three brood mares now, and I've the good fortune to have that half-sister to Gaye Brief which I bought as a foal. When I bought her I was fired with enthusiasm because Gaye Brief had just won the Champion Hurdle, and so I felt I must have a relation. Phil Sweeney was never really going to part with the filly. But as I had just won the Champion Hurdle with Gaye Brief, he sold it to me – but quite expensively: £15,000 which was a lot of money for a filly foal! It doesn't look expensive now, because she's run three times and she's won twice and she's now tested in foal to Buckley. He's a young stallion by Busted and belongs to my son-in-law. He was a good horse on the flat trained by Luca Cumani and retired sound.

On Administration and Finance 9

I've said on numerous occasions that the Jockey Club does a very good job. Weatherbys at Wellingborough – when you think of the thousands of horses they have 'on their books' – is extremely well run. I went to an open day in the early 1980s, to be taken round and shown how it all works and was most impressed with it. I believe it has got even better now. I've always found Weatherbys and the Jockey Club very helpful. If ever I wanted to know something or had been in a muddle, and rang them up, they always did their best to sort it out for me. Certainly I've not found them unhelpful, anyway.

In the days when Fred was training, Weatherbys were more autocratic. They've become very much more civilised in the last ten years. But even today if, as a trainer, you make an error, you're going to get fined for it. I always wonder why the trainers always get fined for every single error they make, yet Clerks of Courses can guide horses the wrong way and send them head-over-heels over bollards and onto the wrong course so that races have to be declared void. Yet Clerks of Courses don't seem to get penalised very much at all; and they should be.

At Chepstow several years ago, I had a runner in a mares' novices chase, and the dolls were put up so that the runners were sent onto the wrong course. Eventually the race was declared void. And they sent them the wrong way at Goodwood recently. I don't think the authorities rap Clerks of Courses' fingers enough. They should be more careful. They're very keen on fining trainers hefty fines for any slight error. What is good for one should be good for the other.

Clerks of Courses vary tremendously. The main grumble about them is that some have got no imagination whatsoever in the way they frame their programmes. They have the most stupid races. Others do not give you a true account of the going. And that really

is vital, because if you're told the ground is good, and you get to a meeting and find it's firm, you might with a struggle escape without a fine if you don't run your horse. But by and large they're going to fine you. It's expensive enough to take the animal to the meeting without getting fined on top of it. That is all wrong. You're not going to take a horse to a meeting a hundred miles away unless you *intend* to run him, and you're going to run him if the ground is right. If you don't run him, there is obviously a very, very good reason. And that reason is the going. Because if the horse has an ailment you have got the veterinary surgeon to give you your excuse. Therefore it is completely wrong to keep passing out these hefty fines when Clerks of the Courses give you a false report on the going. It's they who should be fined.

It would be very difficult to find a way in which Clerks of Courses could measure the going in a way which everybody would accept. They have that machine in France, and I believe they've tried it over here, but it doesn't seem to work out very well. It's not only that courses do not give you the correct going; some courses have had a lot of wear and tear so they have got no cover, and you are really galloping on mud. That bakes in a matter of a few days, so there is no give in that at all. And Clerks always err on the side of saying the going is better than it is because they want a quantity of runners. It's as simple as that.

I would think the Jockey Club have the right people. The Senior Stewards over the last ten years have been excellent. They've a young Senior Steward now, the Marquis of Hartington. I sat next to him at lunch during the winter at Ascot one day, and thought him most knowledgeable and switched on. I'm sure he'll make an excellent Senior Steward.

This new chief executive will have a very difficult job. I thought it really wanted someone in his mid-forties who'd had some racing experience, either as an owner or as a rider, and also obviously administrative experience. The right person would be difficult to find.

The only really bad stewarding decision that I recall recently was the Ascot Gold Cup with Royal Gait. I wasn't at the meeting, so I only saw it on television. But it did seem to me to be the wrong decision. But the stewards obviously have a much closer view, a slow-motion view, and a view from head-on and sideways. They must have thought they reached the right decision. But to me it looked the wrong one.

Receiving the Gold Cup from the Marquise D'Aulan, wife of the Chairman of Piper-Heidsieck after Royal Frolic's win in the 1976 Gold Cup.

I think the controversial rule where the horse gets disqualified if the jockey rides recklessly or carelessly is a bit unfair, too. By and large you should stand the jockey down for a day, but the horse should keep the race unless he's absolutely knocked another one over!

Fred thought stewarding was quite good. I never remember hearing Fred grumble about the stewards: he thought they did a good job. His main grumble about the administration of racing was about Clerks of the Course: about them giving false going accounts, and also that their programmes aren't properly drawn up.

All the Clerks of the Courses ought to get together to try and work out programmes so that they don't, for example, have all condition races in one week – and then none for several weeks – as they do have at the moment. They should allot them month by month. They could get together and have a meeting a couple of times a year, before they printed their programmes. Weatherbys should see that they do.

The planning committee should get all the Clerks of Courses together and go through every programme, race by race, so that you don't get the same races with the same conditions in one week. You need to thin them out. You should have one in the north and one in the south. Now you get three stayers' condition hurdles in a fortnight, and then none for two months! It's the same thing with condition chases. The public will always go to see a good horse, a horse with a name, who runs in condition chases. In National Hunt racing, the horses have been around for a long time. The public know them. They associate themselves with a particular horse, and they go and see it run, no matter where it runs, even in a small field.

This is a very character-istic photograph of Fred taken after he had won the Grand National. The little man peeping over his shoulder appears in many photographs of Grand National winners and no one knows how he ever used to get in with the connections!

In the condition races in jumping, you're going to get your Desert Orchids winning. In your hurdle races, you're going to get the Champion Hurdler – like Toby Balding's Beech Road. But those stars can't win them all. If condition races were spread out during a season, you would give your horse who just misses the very top class a good chance of winning one of them. At the present moment, your horse that just misses top class is always getting beaten by your one very good horse, the Desert Orchids over fences, the Beech Roads over hurdles.

With more condition races, if the star chose to run this week, he couldn't run next week. Your ones not quite in the top flight

119

would have more opportunities, because in a handicap they have got virtually no chance. They are handicapped right out of it over hurdles. Not so much over fences, because somehow or other, three-mile chasers seem capable of giving the weight away. I can't tell you why, but they always have done. I don't think it's because they're bigger, stronger animals. I think it's because there are so very few horses who genuinely stay three miles. That could be the answer. Lots of horses win over three miles because the opposition isn't too good, but they're probably not genuine three-mile horses.

I also feel very strongly that prize money is distributed wrongly. By and large it is a disgrace. There is a sixty/forty division for flat racing/jumping. Yet you see a flat race with twenty or thirty thousand pounds added with only three or four runners. You'll have one horse which is probably three to one *on*. And yet the Levy Board have supplied a certain amount of that money.

How can the punter get any enjoyment out of it at all? He can't, because he can't have a bet. And the punter wants to have a bet. If everybody is so keen on looking after the punters, then they should cater for them. You can give the punters more chance of betting in big handicaps, big novice and maiden races.

We haven't had travel allowances for a long time. They were a tremendous help. But presumably if we had them again they would have to come out of the Levy. It would be better to give that money in prize money, rather than in travel allowances, in spite of the fact that it's very expensive to travel horses today. Once you leave the yard, it is an expensive proposition. Travel allowances might get more runners and therefore more betting.

Why are you having so few runners on the flat in mid-season? The ground may be firm but it's acceptable to the flat race people. A walk-over seems ridiculous for a two-year-old race or a three-year-old race in the summer. That again is an instance of wasting money. And it isn't happening just occasionally. You get the odd walk-over jumping in the autumn when the ground is very hard, but those are very few and far between. But you shouldn't get it in the middle of the flat race season.

On the whole question of money in racing, I think almost everybody agrees that the bookies should contribute more. How do we make them contribute more? Doesn't the Home Secretary have the final say? The bookies have to have a licence, I presume. If they don't contribute X%, they don't get a licence. It's as simple

as that. I am sure they could afford to contribute much more. Why are the big bookmakers so keen on buying up the little ones? They've gobbled most of the little ones up. So presumably they must be making money. And therefore they should contribute more to racing.

I'm not in favour of having no bookmakers at all. I never was, because I hate racing in France. It's a soulless situation. You leave the paddock in France, and you wander out and it is absolutely dead. It's horrid. I am absolutely certain that the bookies create the atmosphere. It's a possibility to have bookies on the course and the tote off the course, like the Australian method, which I imagine is a good one.

If I were the Margaret Thatcher of the racing world I would straightaway do what I've said about the bookmakers. I'd make it so that there were only on-course bookmakers. Off-course there would be a tote monopoly. Therefore you would have so much more money to plough back into racing, so the prize money would go up, the owners would get more, and the lads would earn more.

In the Winners' Enclosure at Cheltenham after Royal Frolic's Gold Cup win. Fred with Ben McCabe, then the horse's lad whom Fred later picked to be our excellent head lad.

121

Rag Trade in the Winners' Enclosure after winning the Grand National. On the left touching the sheet is our famous travelling head lad, Jack Kidd. Fred walking across to the right. On the far right you can see the horse's owner, Teazy-Weazy Raymond. I am at the horse's head. The horse's lad (dark hair, mackintosh, back to us holding him) is Kevin Bishop who was with us for 31 years and was a very good schooling jockey and rode winners himself.

It would be better for everybody. The only people that wouldn't be so well off would be the bookmakers!

The Jockey Club are pleased to have suggestions. They are certainly not opposed to listening, if you put forth a suggestion. I'm not saying they will always act on it, but they are prepared to listen. A lot of people around have a misguided idea that they won't; they do. I wrote to them about the clashing of meetings. They wrote back saying, thanks very much, they'd look into it.

I don't know whether we have the right man for the job as racing's supremo. Other sports have chief executives these days, but we never had one in racing. Racing really is much better run by amateurs. It's been run very successfully by amateurs for generations. A lot of people have advocated more professional stewards. I'm certain that's not right. They do have two professional stipendiary stewards there anyway to guide the amateur stewards. It's a thankless task being a steward: you're going to get shot at in all directions. We're all human, and make mistakes, and when the stewards make the occasional mistake there's such a hullabaloo in the papers about it. When they reach good decisions

122

nobody bothers about it as Sheikh Ali said to me one day, 'If a dog bites a man it isn't news, but if a man bit a dog it would be news.'

I certainly wouldn't close any courses. That would be a great mistake. The whole beauty of British racing is the variation of the different courses, left-hand, right-hand, and the undulations. It would be awful to spoil all that. You'd reduce it to American-type racing, like dog racing. It would be completely and utterly wrong. You must have the variations. That's the beauty of British racing. That's why it's so popular.

I view the prospect of all-weather racing with horror! A week at Southwell is mind-boggling. If they've got all that money to invest in a new course, they should invest in some 'under-floor' heating on two or three tracks to try out as they have on football pitches. It wouldn't be easy. One track wouldn't stand the wear and tear: they'd cut it to ribbons. But if some thought was put into it, and they selected the right tracks, and didn't overdo the number of days racing, but had a month between meetings, something could be worked out.

The facilities on some of the racecourses are awful. You could attract more people by making courses much more comfortable. People who go racing in the middle of a week are usually retired people, because most people are earning their living five days a week. We need to give them a bit more comfort, places where they can go and sit, have a cup of coffee or a drink. Somewhere simply to sit down, somewhere where you've not got to fight your way into the bar to get a drink, nor fight your way to get a cup of coffee, and when you've got it you've got nowhere to sit and study your paper.

I would certainly have pitched the Levy far higher, I can tell you. Look at Australia for example, something like four per cent. It's scarcely one per cent over here. It's a disgrace, an absolute disgrace. All the big bookmakers are so rich, it isn't true. And everybody else in racing is struggling. So the bookmakers are just living off trainers, the owners and the jockeys. I don't feel so badly about the on-course bookmakers, because at least they are there, and they do make a genuine book. But these wretched betting-shops where they're paying nothing to the racecourse directly, I think are monstrous.

I hardly ever have a bet, so I'm not speaking as a gambling person. I'm virtually a non-gambler. But bookmakers on course do create an atmosphere; without it a meeting is soulless.

123

If we had more money coming back into racing from book-makers, I would certainly put a lot into prize money which then would filter right down and you would be able to pay your lads a higher wage. The percentages would be much higher when they had a winner, the owners would be better off, and if they're better off the jockeys are better off and the lads are better off. It would work straight down the scale.

I wouldn't think of payments direct to stable staff in smaller unsuccessful yards. They have direct payments already from the percentage deducted from every win, which comes to trainers who then pass it on to the stable staff. Then you have to send a return back to Weatherbys so that they know exactly who's had what, which is quite right.

I wouldn't be in favour of direct payments to stables regardless of winners, because the more winners you have the more incentive your lads have got. If you've got a good yard and good horses, you'll always get good lads. They may say in Newmarket that the Cecils and Stoutes not only cream off the best horses but cream off the best lads. Very likely. Lads will want to go and work in the successful yards. It's always been the same. If the prize money was increased the basic wage of stable lads would be increased. But to say you should spread any extra money around direct to lads in unsuccessful yards is just not on. I would definitely call myself an élitist. If you prove yourself good enough you get more of the cake.

Who are you running racing for? Are you running it for the punters who put nothing into it, or are you running it for the owners, who carry all the costs? It should be run for the owners, they carry the cost. You don't *have* to have a bet. If you do have a bet, then you abide by the rules as they are laid down. No, I haven't got any sympathy for punters at all. I never had. The owners pay for their horses to be trained, they pay for the jockeys to ride them and they pay extortionate entrance fees. But the punter is free to have his bet or not to have his bet, and he must accept the result and the consequences. So my sympathy isn't with the punter.

On The Media and Press   10

Unless you're meeting success or disaster, the press don't want to know you. If something horrible looks like happening, or has happened, they never stop ringing you up. Or if something really good has happened, they never stop ringing you. Otherwise they don't really bother with you. That's a bit the same in any walk of life.

You have to talk to the press and say something to them, otherwise they can be very difficult. Fred was very good with the press and had many good friends in them, principally Peter O'Sullevan, who's remained a good friend of mine. By and large, I got on with the press pretty well, what dealings I've had with them. There's only one I didn't get on with very well and that's Julian Wilson, but most people know that anyway. I have a feeling – if you watch him interviewing somebody – that he's always poking round trying to dig something out. Maybe that's the secret of being a good journalist, but it's much nicer to be interviewed by any of the others than by him.

I wouldn't say that I'm particularly fond of the press, but I get on perfectly well with them. I don't think there have been any I'd openly avoid and wouldn't bother speaking to. Some obviously you prefer to others, but you have that in any profession. There are some people you like and admire, and other people you're not so keen on, no matter what you do in life.

In the racing press, the outstanding one is Peter O'Sullevan. He was first-class, head and shoulders above them all, but he's retired now. He was wonderful as far as television was concerned, because he's a wonderful race-reader. In the days he wrote for the press I think he wrote a very good column. George Ennor now writes very well for *The Racing Post*: when he covers a race he gives you a pretty true description of it. I read quite a lot of racing journalism. Some styles do turn me off completely, but I read

Comedy of Errors ridden by Ken White jumping the last to win his second Champion Hurdle, 1975. This was the best horse that we ever trained at Kinnersley and he proved it with the races he won.

OPPOSITE
Connaught Ranger being led in after winning the Erins Food Hurdle at Leopardstown in 1979 (Colin Tinkler up). That season he also won the Berkshire Hurdle at Newbury. He is being led in by his owner's wife Mrs McCoughey and head lad Ben McCabe. In the background is Professor Martin Byrne who was a great help to us when looking at horses.

them. I wouldn't be human, if I didn't. I read what they say about my horses when they ran, and now I read with interest what they say about other people's horses.

I'm not terribly keen on Geoff Lester's style of journalism to be quite honest – he's the 'lead-writer' in *The Sporting Life*. I think possibly he doesn't know very much about a horse as a *horse*. He probably writes a column all right, but regarding knowing anything about a horse, I think his knowledge is pretty limited. But he probably describes a race all right, which, when all's said and done, is what they're paid to do, I suppose!

Of the TV people like McCririck, you have him for what he is. To me he's a complete waste-of-timer and, I think, a bore. But I suppose there are quite a lot of people who watch racing who may quite enjoy him. I think Channel 4 otherwise have a very good team –Brough Scott is excellent – and they give you a very good coverage. I prefer the Channel 4 to the BBC coverage because with the BBC on a Saturday, they've barely got past the post, before they've switched you onto swimming or athletics or something. The BBC always seem to keep interrupting with something.

SIS is a tremendous boon, but I don't know who can afford to

126

have it apart from racecourses and betting shops. I suppose some people can. Any racing on television is a boon: it brings it into people's homes.

The coverage that races like the National get sometimes means a lot of stupid criticism. Some of the horses that ran and got into trouble in the National shouldn't have been running in it. That amateur shouldn't have ridden in the race in 1989 and his horse shouldn't have been running in it. Whatever sport you participate in you're going to have accidents, because it's a high risk sport, whether it be motor racing, eventing or racing.

But if they would like to publicise the horrific way that some horses and ponies are kept in one miserable little field half-starved, they would show that a horse is jolly lucky to be a *racehorse*, I can tell you that.

On Whips 11

The press and media people make a ridiculous fuss about this whipping business. Most of them have never ridden a horse in their lives. They probably couldn't keep a bicycle straight. And the people who write in to complain after watching a race on television, can't tell what's really happening either. Jockeys' arms whirling about may look bad, but, unless you know, you can't tell if the horse is even being touched. There's an awful lot of rubbish talked and written.

But it's the 'anti's', as I call them, who in this day and age, always make the biggest noise – it's the same with the anti-hunting brigade. Very few jockeys abuse a horse. Very few trainers would let them. It's the press who stir up all the fuss.

The limit about the number of times was laid down to guide the local stewards I suppose. 'Ten strokes from the last', they say. But you can't lay down strict rules. Ten's probably too much most times, but you can get two horses locked together in a desperate finish which makes things different.

Jockeys generally shouldn't hit a horse with the whip approaching a fence or a hurdle, because it unbalances it. You should put your whip down approaching a fence or a hurdle, and ride him with your hands and your heels. Most good jockeys do that. They wouldn't be hitting them hard at that last stage of the race, because if they did the horse would lose his concentration and probably fall. So they'd be defeating their object. A 'reminder' wouldn't do them any harm. But if you really hurt the horse he'd lose his concentration and he wouldn't jump it well.

All the boys used to ride out with a stick at home, but they hardly ever used them. We never actually taught them how to use the whip. That's a thing that comes naturally, if you can ride. You give a horse a slap down the shoulder, that's all you ever do, unless you had a horse that was really misbehaving, and it probably would want a couple of smacks.

129

The Queen Mother's Private Secretary, Sir Martin Gilliat, sent us this amusing photograph of Fred and him at Newbury after a race. Fred is kindly holding the Queen Mother's handbag at Sir Martin's request while she made a presentation.

Over the years we don't seem to have had any of those sort of horses. Horses generally have got much more amenable. You hear horrific stories from the olden days about these 'unrideable' horses and all that sort of thing. But I can't remember having a horse like that for years. Whether it is that they're better broken now, or whether it is that they're handled more now when they're young – I can't tell. But certainly you don't have the sort of rogue horse that one used to hear about in the olden days.

I most definitely would not support any idea for banning whips. Very rarely have I thought any of our jockeys' use of the whip was excessive. On the odd occasion, I've said to a rider, 'You've knocked that horse about a bit unnecessarily', but not for a very long time.

Using the whip in a race should be a discretionary thing. Occasionally you get a jockey who hasn't had a lot of experience. As a steward, you should say, 'My God! He's not doing that horse any good. We ought to have him in and question him.' But most of the good, regular jockeys today never use the whip excessively.

What made all that come to a head was the year the Irish came over to Cheltenham and seemed to be beating everything excessively. That blew the whole thing up. And the Irish *do* use their whips a lot more than the English riders. You *do* see them using their whip to excess. That's what made everybody 'trigger-happy' and the public went overboard then, like they do about a lot of things!

A steward should have sufficient experience to be able to say 'He's knocked that horse about unnecessarily. We'll have him in', or 'Leave it alone.' The stewards have all got race-glasses. You've got a stipendiary steward there to help them and they should be able to use their own discretion about it. I don't think there's any question really about counting how many times they've hit a horse. If you are used to race-reading, you can see if anybody's knocked a horse about, and the stewards should be quite capable of doing something about it. This guide-line about ten strokes is ridiculous.

Terry would not have won the Irish Sweeps on Normandy if he hadn't picked his whip up. I'm perfectly sure that Lester Piggott wouldn't have won the Derby on The Minstrel if he hadn't given him a very hard race. Yet The Minstrel went on and won top class races after, and so did Normandy. Those are two races that stick in my mind where the jockey has used his whip.

The whip question is a very contentious question because there are right ways and wrong ways to use it. That's the point. Experts can tell. The general public almost certainly can't.

12   *On Gambles and Cheating*

It's well-known we were never a gambling stable and Fred was not a real gambler. He loved to have a bet, but he'd never have more than £25 or £50 on a horse, which in those days was much more than it is today.

The first big gamble that we ever brought off as trainers, was for a book maker called Percy Thompson for whom we trained one or two good horses, and he had a very good horse called Ballandine. For his first run we had him in a hurdle race at Worcester, of all places, and Fred told Thompson that he thought the horse would win. 'Oh, I'll send you one of my men down,' said Thompson.

Fred retorted, 'Don't send any of those gangsters of yours. Send someone that isn't known, otherwise we shall get no price about this horse.'

The man who came was Willy Carter, who subsequently turned out to be a professional gambler and would have been the equivalent of a sort of later Alec Bird. Pat Watts, wife of Bill Watts, the Yorkshire trainer who won the Arlington Million, is Carter's daughter. That was the first time that Carter had done a big commission. I shall always remember it.

In the early 1950s Tim Vinall rode Ballandine, a beautiful chestnut horse. We went in the ring and he was twelve to one. Our instructions from Thompson were to put £6,000 on him, a tremendous sum then. Carter said to Fred, 'I'll go to the one end and you start at the other.' I'm an absolute idiot regarding the gambling because I've never done it, but Carter and Fred started at either end of the line of bookies and started betting. They managed to get £4,000 on the horse. Ballandine duly won as expected and was returned at six to one. Fred rang up Thompson in the evening rather apologetically and said, 'I'm afraid we couldn't get it all on.' But Thompson was thrilled. 'I didn't think you'd got *any* on,' he said, 'when I saw he was at that wonderful price.'

That huge sort of gamble scared the living daylights out of us as far as gambling was concerned. We didn't really ever train for anyone else who had a bet to that extent, except for Bob Jelliman, who was a carpet manufacturer from Kidderminster. He had two quite good horses, Fordham and Salvo. Fordham had run in the Derby, he was a high class ex-flat race horse and Salvo was the same type. They both won for him, but he also backed them when they got beaten, and he got into trouble gambling. He used to walk down the line of bookmakers and they used to see him coming and shorten the price.

You read in the press, and you hear more often on racecourses of horses being given 'easy races' and that sort of thing, to get them ready for a gamble. But quite honestly it doesn't happen very often. I think since I held a licence there was only one horse that I gave a run to deliberately. It was a horse at Nottingham called Papa's Buskins, and it belonged to a wild, mad, Irishman who wanted to have an enormous bet on it. I gave it a run at Nottingham just to give it a canter round, to see how it was going, as I knew nothing about the horse.

So it had a run at Nottingham and then we took it to Haydock and the Irishman did have an enormous gamble on it. And it did win. There was a horse in the race that young Michael Dickinson was training which was favourite. So there was a ready-made favourite in the race for me, to give us a price, because I knew this man was going to have a lot of money on.

Sam Morshead rode the horse at Nottingham, and gave it a quiet race, and then when it won at Haydock, the man won a fortune. That is the only time that I have run a horse since I've held a licence that I think in my heart could possibly have won and didn't. And I don't even know that he could have won at Nottingham. But he could have been quite a bit nearer.

Stories of cheating in jumping are grossly exaggerated. What they do on the flat I can't tell, but most jumping horses run on their merit. There are certain occasions when you have a nice young horse which you don't want to have a terribly hard race the first time it runs. But that's accepted. It's rather like, I imagine, on the flat having a very nice two-year-old and not giving it a terribly hard race first time out. But as for deliberately stopping a horse that was capable of winning, I think those occasions in jumping are very few and far between. Of all the runners I had, anyway, I've never had a horse that I was *sure* could have won that didn't.

Nor do I know of anyone else stopping horses that would certainly have won. You've got the Martin Pipes of this world. Would he have more than two hundred winners in a season, if he was stopping anything? He wouldn't. That applies to most stables. They all want winners. There's always the exception to every rule, but by and large most horses today are run on their merits. With a nice young horse that you didn't want to have a hard race first time, you'd say to your jockey, 'Win if you can, but don't knock him about, don't give him a hard race.'

But 'deliberately stop a horse'? Those occasions, as far as I was concerned, were non-existent.

There was a bit more of it in the past. In the year before the war when Fred first became champion jockey, his brother-in-law, Gerry Wilson, had already been champion for the six previous years. Fred was fighting hard to beat him for the championship. One day they were both at Haydock. There were about four runners in the race and Gerry said to Fred, 'I've got you a spare ride in the first.'

Fred said, 'That's fine, I'll ride it.'

Anyway, he was changing and getting into the colours when Gerry came up to say, 'Now, you stop this horse. Just give him a canter around. I've put you in for the ride, remember. *My* horse is the fancied one.'

When Gerry had gone Fred turned to his valet, who was an old man called Roberts and exclaimed, 'Stop it! Will I hell!' He went out to ride the horse which was called Man in the Moon. It had only one eye and was trained by a man called Hollowell. When Fred walked into the paddock, Hollowell said, 'Now, just give this horse a nice quiet race. Gerry's is the one that's fancied.'

Fred won. Afterwards Hollowell said, 'What am I going to tell my bookmaking friends?'

Fred snapped, 'I don't give a damn what you tell them!'

That's one of the occasions when Fred rode a winner when he wasn't supposed to, and one of the occasions when he was asked to stop a horse. By and large Fred wouldn't ever stop a horse and that story goes to prove it.

I held a licence for eight years after Fred died, and I never stopped a horse. I've never had one good enough, despite the fact that I won Champion Hurdles and races at the National Hunt Meeting. 'Stopping' is something which people who write just love to say!

Jack Kidd, probably one of racing's most famous travelling head lads, with one of his horrific brood of cats! He lived in the yard at Kinnersley for 30 years, having introduced himself to Fred down the telephone. It was a great blow to me when he died.

Gerry Wilson, six times champion jockey and certainly the most wonderful horseman, as opposed to being a jockey, always said he only once stopped a horse in all the years that he rode, and that, too, was at Nottingham. When he got right up the far side, where you start to turn the bend after passing the stables, he quickly pulled it up, jumped off, and undid the girths. And then said the saddle had slipped. You couldn't do that today with the video watching! As he always said that was the only time he ever stopped a horse, that goes to show you that racing, even in those days, was virtually very much straighter than a lot of people would have you believe.

On Sickness 13

Fifteen years ago nobody ever heard of 'The Virus'. I feel the virus only came to us through the international exchange of horses. That's progress, but unfortunately not in the right direction. One didn't have 'the virus' in the old days. The horses would cough, have runny noses and probably run temperatures for twenty-four hours. But in three weeks they had recovered.

Yet with the virus, the horses in many cases, don't show any symptoms until you put them on a racecourse. They appear well, they eat well, they look well and they feel well. But when they come under pressure they can't go through with it. We had every horse endoscoped the day before we ran him and took his temperature. The endoscope is the only thing that really will tell you. Several other trainers do the same thing. It's a tedious job, but at least you know their lungs are clear.

We had a very good horse called Inisharran who had the virus, and who didn't really recover. He ran at Ascot once and burst a blood vessel badly in both nostrils. He was a horse with a world of ability. He won several races, but he never ever recovered from the virus. He never came back to what he should have been. He was a top-class and beautiful horse but he never came really right again. He was always prone to burst blood vessels.

I don't think anybody has got to the bottom of the virus. They swear in America that they don't have it. I was at one of the big equine centres in Virginia, talking to one of their top vets who said, 'We don't have the virus!'

I always thought blaming ailments on farming practices was pretty doubtful. It's only a possibility. Other yards have had the virus; big yards which are nowhere near fields of oil-seed rape, or crops that have been sprayed. Newmarket yards have it. If you get the virus, it's a matter of luck as much as anything. People do everything they can for it nowadays: they try dust-free bedding,

These two horses have won three Champion Hurdles. On the edge of the gallops up near The Panorama I am riding Comedy of Errors who was my hack for 10 years. On the right is Gaye Brief whom I trained to win the 1983 Champion Hurdle. Here he is ridden by his stable girl, Cynthia Corbett. Note how different they are in physique, Gaye Brief being a slight, high-class quality horse whereas Comedy really looks like a three-mile chaser.

and masses of fresh air. Really you can't do much else.

Of course, horses pick up dreadful things off the land. Woodland Venture died after being grazed on some old sheep areas with a thing called Black's Disease, a type of liver-fluke which sheep get. It's very unusual for a horse to get it.

We bought Royal Frolic at Doncaster Sales, as an unbroken three-year-old after he'd been turned out on some very wet pasture in Ireland. We won a race with him as a four-year-old, but after that he just went to nothing. We had him tested for almost everything and found he'd got liver-fluke. They all said it was because he'd been on this bog land in Ireland and the liver-fluke, I would imagine, had been lying dormant for about a year.

You hear many horrific stories about this herpes virus which they unfortunately had at a well-known stud. I saw a video of some of the mares there at a T.B.A. meeting and they looked absolutely terrible. They suffer paralysis. But they got the better of it in the end. They mastered it and the stud reopened.

138

Over the last five years I was training, two horses had the virus and never recovered. I wouldn't like to name them. Other trainers tell you the same thing. I was talking to Fred Winter one day, and he said, 'I've had eight or nine with the virus and they'll never recover.' If they are young horses, they might get their form back in a couple of years' time, but it knocks them sideways.

If you have the misfortune to get the virus and you run them and they burst a blood vessel, they possibly don't recover. Yet you see other horses who recover. I remember a very good horse, Slalom, who burst a blood vessel at Ascot. One immediately thought, 'Well, that's polished him off.' But he turned round and won a very competitive race at Liverpool, so he had obviously recovered.

All horses are as individual as human beings. Some it affects very much worse than others. Others will shake it off and get over it, but you do get the odd one or two who will never get over it.

With jumping horses, leg trouble is the most common ailment.

A lovely action shot of Gaye Brief at Ascot with Sam Morshead up.

139

Gaye Brief having beaten Dawn Run in the Templegate at Aintree on Grand National Day, 1983.

But I'm not in favour of firing. Gay Trip got leg trouble and recovered, but he was never bar-fired: he was only acid-fired. We had no horse bar-fired at Kinnersley for thirty years. Fred didn't agree with it and I don't either. Acid-firing isn't painful. You can pin-fire a horse and that's not painful. But I wouldn't have a horse bar-fired: that went out in the Dark Ages.

Gay Trip was just acid -fired. You can acid-fire them today, and tomorrow they can be loose in a box and within three days they can be let down and be perfectly all right. Rest is the cure as much as anything. If you have a horse with leg problems, you've got to make up your mind that it's going to be twelve months off the road and give it the rest. Fred used to say 'You might as well

140

blister his back!' That meant you couldn't ride him for six months and so he was saying, 'You can't expect to wave a wand and treat a horse and within six months they'll be running.' There are odd occasions when people have got away with it, but by and large they need twelve months.

We never tried the carbon-fibre implant for any of our horses, but I had the new injections done on a couple. It will be interesting to see how they work out. The theory is that they work long-term for four or five months injected by needle. The type of fluid is like that used to treat human beings with varicose veins. The thing is in its infancy. It's been used on a few horses successfully, but nothing is ever always successful with horses. That's why, when you're buying a young horse, you must look at its pedigree and make sure it's a sound family. It's like a healthy family of human beings: you want to look very closely at the pedigree. I'd prefer to buy stock by a stallion who's raced until he's four or five, so that he's sound, not one of these 'injured' things, that's been retired to stud immediately he's three.

I know that if you've got a very high-class horse, the stud value is so terrific they almost have to retire them. But for a jumping stallion who's retired when he's three – he's obviously had a problem. So you're breeding from something that isn't sound. No matter what you pay for a horse today, it's going to be expensive. It costs just as much to keep a bad one as it does to keep a good one. So you want to try and set off with everything on your side and in your favour.

We used a 'back man' a lot. Back trouble isn't difficult either to diagnose or cure. If we had a horse that had a fall, we always had the back man to see him, before we ran him again, and it's comparatively easy to tell if he's all right.

Blood tests will show whether you've got muscular damage or bone damage in a horse. But if you know your horses, if you're familiar with them and you see them come out in the morning – he pulls out, or he dips his back or doesn't pull out, one-two-three-four, you immediately say 'He's got a bit of muscular trouble, or he's probably got a bit of back trouble.'

Your boys, your staff, ride these horses every day. We always tried to keep the same riders on the same horses, so they got to know them. Then lads know if they are moving correctly and how they are going.

I swum a little horse called Divine Charger, in my last season. I couldn't get him right. I was sure it was his back, so I sent him down to Bristol University. They X-rayed him from the top of his head to the tip of his tail, and sent him back and said 'We've no idea what's wrong.' They suggested I gave him six months rest. So then Johnnie McConnochie had the bright idea 'Why don't we send him swimming?' So we sent him swimming for a fortnight and he seemed perfectly all right. He's run three times since his problems. He didn't win, but he's run well enough.

Veterinary treatment has improved over the fifty years Fred and I were training, but vets are rather like the human doctors. Nowadays they immediately run for their injections, and that isn't really the answer to all ills. They're very fond of injecting horses for almost everything. But then medicine has improved to such an extent from the old days when you didn't have all these advanced antibiotics. Some horses take a longer time to get over the treatment of a course of antibiotics. It knocks them sideways and to be quite honest, I hate them. But there are occasions when certain horses do have to have them, though I'm sure they take some time to recover.

On Travel 14

In the late 1950s that gallant amateur the Duke of Alburquerque invited some English trainers and amateur riders to take some jumpers out to Madrid to race. Ivor Herbert took two and we took two and there were about six others. Fred, myself and Ivor and Jennifer, who was Ivor's wife at that period, flew out with the horses in the plane. We sat on straw bales at the back.

In those days the plane was unpressurized so it had to fly round the side of the Pyrenees. We had to come down to Bordeaux to refuel. The horses got terribly hot waiting on the airfield which was then quite small. Fred opened the front of the aeroplane and the pilot nearly went on strike and said he wouldn't fly on. We persuaded him to let us give the horses some water. We eventually struggled round the mountains and climbed on towards Madrid – you have to get up very high to get into Madrid.

When we had landed the horses were all put into a sort of cattle truck. Fred being Fred, insisted on going with the horses. It was a jolly good job he did, because somebody had tied one up with the wrong knot, so that it nearly strangled itself, and they had a hair-raising ride out to the racecourse stables.

The horses did quite well. Ryan Price sent one which won, one of ours was third and afterwards the Duke gave a most wonderful ball for the British contingent. There were five hundred guests, and four bands and all the food was produced by the Duke's own staff. All his footmen dressed in his livery were walking about carrying the food on huge silver platters: suckling pigs and chickens and beef, you've never seen such a feast. And they walked in in a procession, like you see in films, at that fantastic ball!

The English contingent were all taken out in a bus. When we came to enter the estate we were stopped at the entrance gates by the Duke's private guards who had machine guns, so that we all

The presentation after Gaye Brief's Champion Hurdle win. Sheikh Ali congratulates me with jockey Richard Linley between us and Mr and Mrs Paddy McGrath of Waterford Crystal, on the left. This was the one meeting where Sheikh Ali always liked to have runners. He said to me afterwards 'This was my greatest thrill racing'.

had to show our credentials showing we were who we said we were. John Lawrence, John Oaksey as he is now, was on the trip.

We had a week there and they entertained us magnificently. We were the guests of the Spanish Jockey Club, and we also had a cocktail party at the British Embassy. They took us out to a stud farm where they rear fighting bulls. John Lawrence and someone else got into the little practice bull ring with some young fighting heifers which they use to breed from – very savage little things.

When we ran Gay Trip in the French National at Auteuil, Terry was to ride. He was always heavy and he hadn't even heard of the word 'waste'! In France you're not allowed to carry more than about two pounds overweight. If not, the trainer has to put up a different jockey who can do the weight. In England you can put up whatever overweight you like. But there you can't, and Terry of course suddenly announced the night before that he was a considerable amount overweight. He said he'd have to spend the night in the Turkish Baths.

Fred said, 'I bet he doesn't,' so he went and spent the night in the Turkish Baths with Terry to make sure that he did and next

144

day Terry carried just the two pounds overweight that he was allowed.

Spartan General ran in the French Champion Hurdle because he belonged to a girl who was a European Water Ski Champion, and whose husband was a World Water Ski Champion, a French boy called Phillipe Lejou. So she wanted Spartan General to run in France, but he didn't run frightfully well. Over the last thirty years the English record of runners in the French Champion Hurdle has been abysmal. Ryan Price won it, and our horse Gaye Chance was third in it, but that's about all.

The French run their races entirely differently to ours. In the French Champion Hurdle, for example, which is three and a quarter miles or thereabouts, when they've gone only a mile and a half, they pick their whips up and go from there! The ground in France is always difficult: it's watered ground, it's false, and it's not nice ground at all. The hurdles are entirely different to ours, like little brush fences. The chase course at Auteuil is definitely difficult. The fences are quite big and they're tricky too. They run up a bank to jump an obstacle and there are some rails coming off it: it's a formidable course.

About twenty-five years ago we started going to Kenya. Fantastic trips. We went on a shooting safari, and lived under canvas in the northern district of Kenya. Fred did actually shoot a buffalo. He wasn't very keen on shooting the game, which you could do then with a licence, and though we went back every year after for years, he never ever tried to shoot another thing. He just didn't want to. One could've done in those days, but he wouldn't. I quite agreed with him. But the buffalos are horrible beasts really, so I didn't mind that being shot.

I'm not at all keen on shooting. Fred was a very good shot and had a gun in Tim Holland-Martin's Overbury shoot for years, but I've never been to a shoot in my life, and although lots of wives go, I never would.

One year we went to the Galapagos Islands. We spent a week going round all the different islands, on an Ecuadorian boat, the only two English people there. Fabulous. We saw all the iguanas, the marine ones and the land ones. One day, Fred somehow or other got talking to the Captain (who couldn't speak any English), but he made Fred understand, 'Would you like to go fishing?' So whilst the rest of us were all trooping miles over the islands, Fred and the Captain made off fishing and caught those big grouper

Gaye Chance ridden by Sam Morshead after winning the Royal Doulton Hurdle Race at Haydock in a snow storm. He won 18 races including the Waterford Crystal Stayers and the Sun Alliance Novices both at the Festival Meeting at Cheltenham. He was own brother to Gaye Brief owned by Mary Curtis. Fred and travelling head lad, Clifford Rawlings, are leading him in.

fish with those big mouths. We swam in the sea with dozens and dozens of sea lions, and seals. It was a marvellous trip and a wonderful experience, but the food was horrendous and the rest of the passengers were nearly all Germans.

We would always rather go on those sort of holidays than go to Barbados – 'Newmarket-on-Sea'. When you're very young a beach holiday appeals to you, because there are so many sports you can take part in. But when you get older you can't. Anyway, I'm much too old to go and lie on the beach now, and see all these glamorous dolly-birds walking up and down.

But we nearly got kidnapped in Kenya by some 'Shiftas', as bandits are called out there. We were going in a Land Rover from one lodge to another and the road was blocked. They had blocked it on purpose. We made a deviation and discovered that one lot of Americans just ahead of us had stopped and got out like

146

Americans would. The bandits stripped them, took everything off them and then left them. We had just missed it, which was lucky.

We used to go up to the Jade Sea which is particularly wild, up on the Ethiopian border. That was always a thrill and an adventure. The heat would be terrific, about 110° and nothing up there but this fabulous lake. We used to go fishing on it and catch Nile perch. It was full of Nile perch and crocodiles. I swam in it – I must have been mad! All those sorts of things, and you're away from the madding crowd.

One day I was riding through the forest near Mount Kenya, with a man who started the Mount Kenya Safari Club, a friend of ours, Brian Burrows. As we were riding down towards a water hole, suddenly a full-grown rhino was facing us. Brian stopped immediately and whispered, 'Sit absolutely still. Don't say a word.' Rhinos have very poor eyesight, but very good smell. I looked a bit further and there was the baby rhino, and it was on its way to its baby. We sat absolutely still; the horses froze automatically. Anyway the mother thudded on down the path, and found its baby, and when she got to it, we were able to turn and go off.

We went to Uganda twice, a beautiful country, and saw all those lovely monkeys, with long silky, black and white fur, in the rain forest. We went to the Murchison Falls. The fish come over the falls and the crocodiles squat there waiting, because they're so lazy, waiting to eat them as they come over. We stayed at Chobi Lodge up at the Falls. I think those lodges have all gone, and they've probably killed most of the animals.

We went down to the coast and we stayed in a tiny place called Indian Ocean Lodge, with only four bedrooms. We were picking up an aircraft to fly from Malindi up to Nairobi to catch our flight for England. Walking into the airport, I saw three helicopters there and I thought, 'That's a funny thing,' and the whole place was all in an uproar. Everybody was fighting to get a seat. We had got our seats booked, but that didn't make any difference. It was the day they tried to have a coup. We got virtually the last plane out of Malindi and the last plane out of Nairobi for the next two or three days. We were in Nairobi the day they shot Mboya. We drove down the next street, unconscious of the fact, and leaving to drive down to the bush.

One place I never want to see again is Cairo! We went on a trip up the Nile, from Luxor to Aswan, one of Fred's bright ideas. I

147

Compare this photograph of Fred in the yard in the late 70s with that on page 18 taken nearly 50 years before. The pollarded lime trees were a feature of the yard at Kinnersley, the theory being that limes attracted flies away from the boxes.

hated it. Cairo was dirty and full of beggars. I rode a camel out to the Pyramids and the Sphinx and was pursued by dozens of beggars and children. I didn't like it at all.

We used to have varied adventures in Northern Ireland. The old Marchioness of Londonderry was a wonderful character. They still had Londonderry House in London, now a hotel, around the corner from the Hilton. We used to go over and stay with them in Mount Stewart in Northern Ireland, a fabulous place, now owned by the National Trust. She would either be in bed or in a chair. She'd always got a huge parrot in her room.

The first time we ever went to Mount Stewart was one August after we'd been to the Show at Dublin. We motored up north with Lady Mairi Bury, old Lady Londonderry's daughter – she's still alive and would probably be younger than me. We walked into this enormous hall of huge flagstones, full of gigantic cages of parrots, and monkeys, and all sorts of things. It was late at night,

148

it wasn't very light, and we were tired. As soon as we walked in, all these things started to screech and squawk. I thought we had gone into a lunatic asylum, but it was a wonderful place to stay.

A very different sort of visit to Northern Ireland was the first time we ever met Crawford Scott (the father of the trainer Homer Scott). He had a horse for sale called Charlie Lad and he asked us to go and see him. We flew to Belfast, and he'd said, 'I'll be standing in the arrival hall wearing a button-hole so you'll know me.' We recognised the man by the button-hole, jumped into his car and off we went.

It was in the early days of the IRA, and they'd just started doing all these terrible things. We were taken all down through the lanes at the back of Armagh and never touched a main road. Suddenly Crawford said, 'You won't mind going round all these back lanes, but we've got a lot of money in the back of the car. Have a look in that shoe box.' I opened the shoe box in the back of the car, and it was full of twenty pound notes. There must have been five or six thousand pounds there.

Going to Birmingham Airport we'd heard on the early morning news that there had been a big IRA find near Armagh on a farm. Crawford asked, 'Did you hear on the news about the IRA arms find?'

We said, 'Yes, we did.'

He said, 'That was on one of my farms, so we're avoiding the main roads in case there's an army road block, because if they find that money in the car they'll think that's an IRA pay off.' The money was for cattle paid in cash because of a bank strike in the South.

We looked at the horse and he continued all down these little back roads and eventually got to Armagh. He parked the car at the back of the bank, and marched off with his money while we had a cup of coffee. The place was absolutely crawling with soldiers. After about twenty minutes, he came out and said, 'Well, that's all right. Now we can go to Dublin.'

We drove out and straight over the border into Dublin, no problem. The horse, Charlie Lad, turned out to be a good horse. We later bought him for Sybil Joseph, Maxwell Joseph's wife, and he won us a lot of races after winning his first race in England for Crawford Scott. Those thousands of pounds would have obviously looked suspect if we'd been stopped. He became a friend, and Homer has remained a friend too.

15 *On Women*

I'm not one of those females who think that females should be able to do everything males can do. There are lots of things females can't do. I don't approve of women riding in open professional races under Rules. But as far as training is concerned, there's no reason why a woman shouldn't do it equally as well as a man. It's not a man's prerogative at all, and I'm not saying that simply because I happen to have been training and been reasonably successful. I just know there's no reason why women shouldn't be good trainers. Women ride competitively in events, and in show jumping. The only thing they shouldn't be doing is riding in professional open races. They are not strong enough. Most women are not as strong as men.

It was Mrs Nagle who took the Jockey Club on and won her case for women to hold trainers' licences. I suppose it would have come in a few years' time because of all the 'Women's Libbers'. But she did the deed, and great credit is due to her for the way she did it, because she fought a good battle without it getting unpleasant, and that's always a very good thing.

Women working in stables possibly have more dedication than men. Talking of my own staff, I had several very good girls, some of whom would certainly be every bit as good as the males and some of them probably would be a bit better. You have the good and bad in every walk of life. But if you get a really good girl, they *are* dedicated, and they do love their horses, possibly more than the man does.

There aren't that many women trainers, though. In jumping you've really only got Mrs Pitman who's in the top flight. I don't know Mrs Ramsden who seems to train a few winners on the flat up North, but Mrs Pitman is the one who springs to mind. Of course, Auriol Sinclair, who trained for years, was a very able trainer, but she had to train under her head lad's name for many, many years.

I think we'll have more and more female stewards. We already have one lady 'stipe', Miss Tonks. She seems perfectly all right as far as I can see.

One of the things that I don't approve of in racing is that they always seem to go for ex-army people. More jobs should be given to people who've worked in racing. One thing which annoyed me very much was the case of John Burke who was a very good rider, and who rode a National winner and a Gold Cup winner for us. When he came to the end of his riding career, he tried to get a job in the 'dope box', helping the dope-testing officials. I spoke to the powers-that-be, and they said 'Yes, we would certainly consider his application.' They did, and in the end he was on the short list of six. But he didn't get it, because it was left to the then senior veterinary surgeon, who gave it to one of his army chums. That is wrong.

They should try where it's possible to give somebody who's given a lot to racing the chance to continue to get a living out of the job, as opposed to giving it to somebody who's never been in racing at all. And that goes for the girls and women in racing, as well, of course.

On The Grand National 16

The course as it is at the moment is excellent. If you modify it any more, you'll take away the National. The fences in the days that E.S.B. and Nicolaus Silver won were very upright and very formidable, but those two were still class horses. Today, any horse that jumps round Cheltenham or Sandown, should jump round Liverpool. But some of the horses running in the National now, quite frankly, have no right to be running in it.

Even more so, I always felt that some of the people who rode in it shouldn't have been allowed to. There should be qualifications for the riders as well as the horses. They have made it into a long handicap, so hopefully you are cutting out the rubbish. I am pleased to say that the Jockey Club has now brought in qualifications for riders. That might remove the 'romantic element of the incompetent amateur', but the accidents they cause are only giving the do-gooders and the anti-bloodsport people opportunities to say what a cruel race the National is.

In actual fact, racing is *not* cruel. If those people went to some of the three-day events – and I've been to quite a few recently watching my grandson – their hair would stand on end. Racing is child's play compared to some of those cross-country courses. Some of the event fences are horrific. You shouldn't ask any horse to do what they're asking them to do.

Whereas in racing, if you have an intelligent horse, if he meets the fence right, he will jump round Liverpool. The greatest hazard in the National is the quantity of runners and loose horses, but you have that hazard in any race. It's simply a bigger hazard at Liverpool because you get more runners.

The last Cheltenham victory of my career. On Thursday, 16 March 1989 we win the Christies Foxhunters with Three Counties ridden by my grand-daughter, Katie. Here we embrace each other after the presentation. This was a real 'Grand-mothers' Horse' since Grandmother Lyons bought the horse for Katie and I chose him and trained him . . .

. . . Katie's father, Guy Rimell, came over from Spain to see this race – an emotional day for the family.

153

17   *On Other Great Horses and Trainers*

I would have loved to have had Persian War, because we came so near to buying him, and then he went and won three Champion Hurdles. When you're under-bidder for something and you just haven't got sufficient money to buy it, and it goes and wins three Champion Hurdles . . . I always followed that horse very closely. I always wished that we'd been able to buy him.

The best chasers I've ever seen were Arkle and Golden Miller. I'd only just started to go racing, and was very naive and unknowledgeable in those days because I was only about fifteen, but I did see the race when Golden Miller and Thomond had that terrific battle in the Gold Cup. It was the first Gold Cup I ever saw, and therefore left an imprint on my mind for that reason, and also because Golden Miller was ridden by Fred's brother-in-law, Gerry Wilson. Golden Miller certainly was a marvellous horse.

Arkle I saw in most of his races. I'm sure we haven't seen anything as good as Arkle since, because Arkle would carry 12st 7lb in handicaps and win them comfortably. At the present moment there's a great shortage of chasers. We just haven't got any. In Arkle's day there were a lot of very good chasers about, whereas today you've got one horse dominating it, Desert Orchid. He's not had many top class opponents. I'm not saying he isn't a good horse. He is; but he's been lucky enough to race in an era when there have been very few good ones to oppose him.

We've been running horses too early and they haven't lasted. People haven't gone in for your old-fashioned chasers, but for the flat-race type of animal, flat-race bred. People haven't had the finance or the patience to wait for them. They'll come back in a few years because people are now breeding more for National

154

Hunt racing. They are realising that National Hunt horses have got a much higher value than they've had in the past.

Look at the prices of National Hunt foals and yearlings, which ten years ago were very small. Today you'd have to give fifteen or twenty thousand pounds for a good National Hunt yearling, and sometimes that for a foal. So therefore people can afford to breed that type of individual which they couldn't before. We'll reap the benefit, and get the better class horse coming on again, and you'll get more good chasers.

Of all the other trainers I've admired over the years, I'd undoubtedly pick out Fulke Walwyn. He was a master of producing his three-mile chasers. His horses always looked well, and I admire him as a trainer more than any other trainer in my time, maybe because I've seen him over so many years, but after all he's had a record number of Hennessy winners. He's obviously not been so successful over the last few years because he hasn't had the horses. He got a bit like me: the horses got thin on the ground, and you can't win races if you haven't got the ammunition.

Here I am in the spring of 1989 standing at the top of our gallops, with some of my cattle. In the background is The Panorama – a folly built for the Coventry family. From it you can see five counties. In the distance stand the Malvern Hills.

But I would say Fulke's a very good trainer and much to be admired. He had patience. And he had the knack of always producing those horses for those big races, both the Gold Cup and the Hennessy. He even won a Schweppes for the Queen Mother with a very bad-legged horse, which couldn't have been easy. He beat us on many occasions, including in the Champion Hurdle with Kirriemuir.

Vincent O'Brien was a marvellous N.H. trainer. His record speaks for itself. But he only brought his horses over for the few big races, whereas Fulke was consistently training in England and therefore you had much more time to assess him. Vincent would just come over and raid Cheltenham and Liverpool. Ryan Price was a master of his art of producing good hurdle-race horses, and his horses always looked very well too, but, I would put Fulke ahead of them.

On Permits and
Point-to-Point Yards

18

Permit holders are taking the livelihood away from the professional trainers. If they are genuine permit holders and they are training genuinely their own horses or their wife's horse or their daughter's horse, then I agree with it. But there are now so many permit holders training horses for other people, which I don't think is right. They are pretending that the horses belong to their family.

And the professional point-to-point yards can't be right either. I always thought that in point-to-points you should own the horse and you should train it yourself. You should not have professional point-to-point yards. Some have twenty-five horses. That is wrong: they might just as well be with a licensed trainer.

That wasn't the intention, but today it has got to the stage where all good point-to-pointers are run from professional yards and are owned by people who are going out and giving twenty or thirty thousand pounds for them. If they want to do that, then they should run them under Rules, and send them to a licensed trainer.

You need a change of rule that says every point-to-pointer must be trained by its owner at home. Just like that. I would slice off the professional point-to-point yards altogether.

19 *On Being a Trainer*

The hardest thing about training horses is to train your owners: the horses are comparatively easy. If you have the good fortune, and it is luck, to know some nice people who want to have horses, then you're quids in. A trainer has got to be a diplomat, a good raconteur, and be knowledgeable about his subject.

Success attracts some of the lesser desirables of the world, who think they are going to get on the bandwagon. The owners who leave you completely alone and allow you to run your horses when and where you want, and when the horses are right, are the ones who are successful. As soon as you get an owner who's got a little knowledge of racing, and they start to interfere, disaster nearly always strikes. You'd be amazed at the people who have owned a horse for a year, and suddenly they've become an authority on racing. Those are the ones that really are a menace.

Nor do you ever want to train for a lot of gambling owners, because it's the age-old story of money and greed. They've only got to have two or three get beaten and they've got to blame somebody. It's never that their horse isn't good enough; it's either that the jockey is at fault, or that the trainer is a fool and has run it in the wrong race at the wrong meeting. Then they take the horse elsewhere. The owners really are difficult. Luck plays an enormous part in racing, as it does in life anyway, but you do have lucky owners and unlucky owners. Obviously you want to train for the lucky owners, but you're not going to know whether they're lucky or not until you've had them for a couple of years.

Under-work your horses rather than over-work them. Try to run your horses in lower company. You can always go up. Don't set off at the top. We had every reason to think Celtic Chief was a very good horse. But the first time I ever ran him was at Newton Abbot in a race for horses that had never run on the flat, so I started him off in the lowest possible company. He belonged to a

Katie in the yard at Kinnersley on her Christies Foxhunters winner, Three Counties. I am giving her a few last minute instructions!

man who had only one horse, not a gambling owner, but who did like to have one decent bet on the horse the first time he was fancied. The first time we ever ran him was in that little race at Newton Abbot, he backed him, and we won. So we started him off at the bottom and he finished up being third in the Champion Hurdle the following season and second in 1989. That shows you how you can go upwards.

Don't fly too high, if you can possibly avoid it. Some of your owners wouldn't see it that way. They buy a horse and want to run at the big meetings, and if you said, 'Let's run at Newton Abbot or Bangor,' they'd shudder and think, 'I haven't bought a horse to run at those sort of meetings.' That's the difficulty that you have with owners.

All the staff at Kinnersley in the last weeks of my training life. Left to right: *Tom Howard, Trevor Heath, Katie Rimell, Taffy Parker, Toni Gresham, Dennis Leahy, Ben McCabe, Mathew Shepherd, Mercy Rimell, Roger Jenkins, Adrian Hamill, Vanda Fowles, John McConnochie.*

But you must persuade them to be content to start off small and to work up to something better. In jumping your horse has got to last several seasons. So when you begin, you don't want him to have a hard race. You want him to come back and think, 'Oh! Isn't that fun!' Then hopefully he'll improve. So you try and find as easy a job for him as you can. The same thing must apply on the flat: no matter how good an animal you have, you want him to have an easy race or two. I don't say you're trying to give the horse a run down the track.

You don't want any horse to keep having a lot of hard races, no matter what age he is, because otherwise he won't last. Horses

160

like to win: they know when they've won. If they keep getting beaten, they are going to get fed up with it. Horses really aren't as stupid as everybody thinks they are. Horses are like human beings. Some are a lot more intelligent than others, and when horses are labelled as ungenuine, there's nearly always a reason for it: they've probably got an ailment of some description.

Years and years ago we had a good horse called Kipper Kite who never wanted to start. Fulke Walwyn used to train him, and he never wanted to jump off. Everybody said, 'He's an ungenuine old thing.' But he won us quite a few races and then in the end he was killed at Cheltenham. They did a post-mortem on him and found he had got a crack in the bone that joined up his backbone from his hip bone. It was an old crack which had obviously been there for years, and must have come from a fall when he was quite young. That was the reason why he didn't want to jump off. Once he got going he probably didn't feel it so much and forgot about it. Lots of good horses have got a problem; they've got an ailment which one doesn't know about.

One of the secrets of Fred's success was he never overworked his horses. Possibly our horses were underworked. But they *lasted*. We didn't leave our races at home on the gallops. Fred's father would have done twice the amount of work with his horses as we ever did with ours. Don't overwork a horse, don't run him until he's ready, and try to find an easy race for him for his first two or three races if you can.

Today you're running horses over fences a lot earlier than you used to do, because of the economics of the job, because people just can't afford to buy four-year-olds and keep them until they're six, before they've any hope of winning a race. So you're putting them under a lot more pressure a lot younger than you should do. They haven't matured.

Lots of horses don't mature until they are six, or even seven. Some human beings don't mature until later in life, and the same thing applies to two-year-olds. A lot of two-year-olds are spoilt because they are asked to do something before they are ready. I don't think there should be any two-year-old races: they should wait until they are three. You need to give their bones the chance to mature and settle.

An awful lot of good young horses are spoilt. It's not specifically the trainers' fault, they are probably being pressed to run by their owners. It's not even the owners' fault: they buy a horse to race, not to have it in the stable or in the field for two or three years. But they are often not prepared to wait.

You must have a rapport with your jockey, because if you've got quite a big yard, you're employing a jockey frequently, so he must be somebody that you get on with. It's essential not to have a personality clash. If you only have a few horses, like I had for the last couple of seasons, it matters less because you don't retain a jockey. You can select whom you want. But if you retain a jockey, it's vital you have a mutual liking, for jockeys can be very tiresome, almost as tiresome as the owners.

If you're employing a top jockey, there are only two things that

The end of an era – my 70th birthday with my brother, Crosby Cockburn, at a party I gave at my home at Upton.

you really need to tell him. Either the horse is very straight, he can hurdle well and he's absolutely fit, he's a good jumper and he enjoys being up there. Or this horse barely gets the trip, hold him up and just come there the once. And that's about all you want to tell him.

With Fred dying in the July, I was launched on another new season almost immediately. So I just went on to the best of my ability, the way that Fred would have gone on, and tried to do all the things he would have done. That was the way it was. There was no other way to do it.

The hardest thing I found was communicating with the owners. Fred was marvellous at that. He'd ring people up and have a chat and gossip; he loved it. Fred loved the telephone, anyway, and I never have. He would love ringing the owners, and he was friends with nearly all of them. So they felt part of the operation, which was tremendous. I found that very difficult to do. I found it very difficult to communicate, difficult to talk to them, to discuss things with them.

Fred was a good mixer. It's much easier for a male to mix and to invite people than it is for one solitary female. One always has the feeling that nobody wants to be bothered with one female, particularly when you're old. They just say, 'That's that wretched old woman again' – I may be wrong, but I always have that feeling. Whereas it was totally different when Fred was alive.

But still, when you have any bad news for an owner, you have got to tell them. It is no use putting it off. Obviously it's always hard to ring up somebody and say, 'Your horse has got a leg problem. It won't run for a year, most likely.' That's always difficult. Or if you have a horse that you've planned a race for, and then you think the horse isn't ready or that the horse has had a slight setback, then it's hard to ring them up and tell them.

By and large, most owners are reasonable. Some of them are awkward. But we're all human beings. You manage them, somehow or other. You've got to learn to manage them, anyway. Training is really learning to manage other humans. I think the horses are quite easy!

Racing's become a much more serious business than it was in our heyday. You don't seem to have – but that's perhaps because I'm on my own now – all the parties I remember, like the great one at the Adelphi in Liverpool after Nicolaus Silver won the National, or the one at the pub in Upton after Gay Trip won his with all our local friends. Upton again and the same pub after Rag Trade's: we gave that party, of course, because Rag Trade's owner certainly wasn't going to give us one! When Normandy won the Irish Sweeps and Bryan Jenks and I were fog-bound in England, Bryan rang Fred in Ireland and said, 'Give a party in the Shelbourne and ask whoever you like.' About eleven Hartys appeared and all Jack Doyle's lot. Life was like that then.

That and the fun weeks staying in Devon at Salcombe or Torquay over Newton Abbot's Bank Holiday meetings. Fulke Walwyn and in those days Diana Walwyn, Tim Molony . . . Everybody used to go. There were all sorts of fun and games at the Imperial, Torquay. In those days, one always joined together.

Do I leave racing a better place than I found it after fifty years? I don't want to leave it, it's as simple as that.

Like everything in life, it's progressed. Sometimes progress is good, sometimes bad. As far as racing is concerned, it's progressed very well. The main bad thing in racing today is that the bookmakers syphon off too much money and they put back very, very little. I don't know what money they get from the SIS, but I think that it should have been controlled by the Jockey Club. I'm no authority on high finance, but I feel that a lot of people are getting a lot of money out of racing and putting nothing into it, and that I think is wrong.

But it's a good life. Finding horses, looking at them in fields, seeing one come on and becoming a good one and winning his first race. Winning the big races. Getting on with the staff at home, talking to them about their horses and their plans. Training and watching the horses work in the lovely countryside in the mornings. Riding out old Comedy. The friends one meets on every course. The old friends among the owners. The fun I've had has been very, very good, and the good times have been marvellous.

Index